Commemorating the 2007
Helen Everett Award Honoree

Marge Custis

OPEN THE WORLD
www.humboldtlibraryfoundation.org

EUR

The **Southern Tailgating** Cookbook

The **Southern Tailgating** Cookbook

A Game-Day Guide for Lovers of Food, Football, & the South

Taylor Mathis

THE UNIVERSITY OF NORTH CAROLINA PRESS   CHAPEL HILL

The paper in this book meets the guidelines for permanence
and durability of the Committee on Production Guidelines
for Book Longevity of the Council on Library Resources. The
University of North Carolina Press has been a member of
the Green Press Initiative since 2003.

Library of Congress Cataloging-in-Publication Data
Mathis, Taylor.
The Southern tailgating cookbook : a game-day guide for
lovers of food, football, and the South / Taylor Mathis.
pages cm
Includes index.
ISBN 978-1-4696-1062-7 (cloth : alk. paper)
1. Cooking, American—Southern style. 2. Outdoor cooking.
3. Tailgate parties. I. Title.
TX715.2.S68M3265 2013
641.5975—dc23   2013004073

17 16 15 14 13   5 4 3 2 1

For tailgaters everywhere

Contents

p. 22

pp. 40, 42

Appetizers & Snacks, 59

p. 78

p. 80

Sides, 89

p. 99

p. 111

pp. 123, 124

Main Meals, 121

p. 137

p. 167

Sandwiches & Soups, 175

p. 185

Desserts, 195

p. 210

p. 28

p. 72

p. 187

Sidebars

Acknowledgments

To the tailgaters whom I met throughout my travels, I can't name you all but I'm thankful for all your help.

To Mac Mackie, my agent, thanks for believing in this project from the beginning. To Erika Stevens, thank you for your editing and words of encouragement. To Elaine Maisner and the staff of the University of North Carolina Press, thank you for making this book happen. I appreciate your patience, support, and expertise throughout this process.

To Sean Patton, thanks for a conversation that led to the big idea.

To Dad, thanks for showing me that hard work works.

To Sara, thanks for your love, support, and understanding throughout this process.

To Sally, Mom, thanks for collaborating with me on the recipes. It was an experience I would not trade for anything.

The **Southern Tailgating** Cookbook

Fans outside Neyland Stadium before kickoff in Knoxville, Tennessee

Do you enjoy a mouthwatering buffet of your favorite foods? Is your ideal Saturday one spent with your friends and family? Is there a college or university you feel a loyalty toward? Congratulations! You could become a tailgater.

There's no membership to obtain or test to pass. You have the intangible skills necessary to spend game day tailgating. Now all you need are the tangible skills. Don't worry; you'll learn about those later on in the book. I'll share with you the tools, techniques, and recipes that will lead you to a successful game-day tailgate. Consider this a warning, though: once you start tailgating, particularly in the South, you won't want to stop. On Saturdays in the fall, southern campuses are taken over by century-old celebrations that bring fans by the thousands. When you've finished reading this book, you'll understand why a game day in the South is unlike any other. And as amazing as game days are, none of this could be possible without you, the fan.

I've always admired creative and passionate people. The football fans I met as I was gathering the content for this book at college campuses across the South are exactly that. They love their teams and families and enjoy celebrating both. For three months during the fall, many lucky southerners become college football tailgaters. They pack up their cars, RVs, boats, or buses and make their way to the college campuses of their favorite teams. On game day, they gather with friends and family, dress in sacred colors, and cheer their teams. These pre- and postgame celebrations are for everyone. Tailgating is an activity for all ages, from nine months to ninety-nine years, and it appeals to anyone who loves great food, being around loved ones, and supporting his or her team.

For two and a half seasons, I traveled across twelve states to experience the different game-day traditions, food, and fan bases that make southern tailgating unique. On every campus, there were allegiances to different teams, but all tailgaters shared in the same hospitality that the South is known for. When one tailgater was in trouble, the tent next door gladly lent some extra charcoal or offered a roll of paper towels. I never went hungry and was always asked if I needed a drink or a plate of food. The tailgaters whom I met during my trip always made me feel welcome and showed that same respect to one another.

This book is filled with pictures and stories. The recipes include family favorites and dishes inspired by what I saw tailgaters making and serving at sites across the South. Keep in mind that to tailgate is to entertain; these recipes aren't great just on game day but can be used year-round. Interspersed with the recipes, you'll find sidebars discussing the uniqueness of a game-day atmosphere. Each campus I visited has special and distinctive traditions, but the sociable tradition of tailgating joins fans, families, and friends across the South.

I hope this books leaves you inspired for your next tailgate, backyard barbecue, family reunion, or any other event you're hosting. Remember, you can't control how your team performs on the field. All you can do is throw the best pregame celebration possible. Good luck to you and your team. Happy tailgating!

Tailgating Food Explained

On game day, fans may do anything from cooking a few burgers on a grill in the bed of a pickup to arriving at their tailgating sites with a trailer-sized pig cooker and two whole hogs smoking away. Tailgating spreads will feed anywhere from two people to more than a hundred. A tailgater does all this not out of the comfort of his or her own kitchen but in a parking space on his or her favorite college campus. Tailgaters are more than just fans; they are on-site caterers who host parties with restaurant-quality food in an environment that was never intended to be a kitchen. Hosting these events requires a crafty and thoughtful approach to menu planning.

At a tailgate, guests typically will spend the day standing with a drink in one hand while enjoying the pregame festivities. Have you ever tried cutting up food on a plate while standing, much less while holding a drink? You end up with more food on the ground than in your mouth. If the food you serve isn't in bite-sized portions or has to be cut with a fork, it should be served between a bun, on a stick, or in a cup or a bowl. Any menu items that require a knife to eat should be carved prior to serving.

As host, you'll want to feed everyone who comes to your tailgate. Throughout the day, you may have multiple sets of guests who drop by at any given time. Serving food that can sit for extended periods of time or can be made to order promptly means no guest will go away hungry.

Serving food that can be eaten while standing up and that does not perish quickly is important for planning a successful tailgating menu. The most essential element of your game-day menu, though, is the element of fun. Serve the food that brings you joy to share with those around you. For many tailgaters, showing support for their favorite team via the food they serve and how they serve it makes their game day special. Arkansas fan Wes Shirley told me that for breakfast, "Razorback fans must have either bacon or ham on game day, which is believed to get the spirit of the hog in you." Samantha Fechtel always begins her Texas game days with a burnt-orange-colored breakfast of pumpkin pancakes and mimosas. WVU fan Cindy Coffindaffer always makes blue and gold thumbprint cookies for dessert on game day.

Tailgating menus will vary from campus to campus, but portable, accessible, and fun food is what you'll find on tailgating menus throughout the South. In this book, I'll share with you dishes that will impress your guests and leave them talking about your tailgate for weekends to come. Remember, a tailgate is a form of entertaining. The recipes in this book are great for any picnic, cookout, camping trip, or other entertaining event during which you may be eating outdoors.

Packing for a Tailgate

Storing, cooking, and serving dishes at a tailgate isn't the same as cooking them for a dinner party in your home. When you arrive at the tailgate, usually a spot in a grassy field or a space in an asphalt lot, you'll find no electricity, no running water, no kitchen counter, and no kitchen table. If you didn't pack what you need, it won't be there. Preparation leads to successful on-site cooking.

Preparing your ingredients the night before will save cooler space and time and will help ensure you don't forget anything. Throughout this book, I'll refer to packing ingredients in sealable containers. These can be plastic

Florida fans using a creative approach to arrive at their tailgate

zipper bags, jars, plastic containers, or whatever type of container works best for you.

CHOPPING, DICING, AND CUTTING

For a more enjoyable tailgate, chop, dice, and cut ingredients the night before the game. Game day will be much more enjoyable if you aren't shedding tears from chopping onions while socializing with your friends. Also, there may be weather elements (wind, rain, or snow) that could make preparing ingredients difficult. Store prepared items in labeled, sealable containers. Refrigerate them overnight and transfer them to your tailgate site in a cooler on game day.

MEASURING SPICES, DRY GOODS, AND LIQUIDS

Instead of bringing a five-pound bag of sugar or a whole gallon of milk, measure out dry ingredients and liquids at home. Put the premeasured items in sealable containers to transport them to your tailgate. Tightly seal the containers to prevent spills. On hot days, keep any dairy products, meats, or other items that need refrigeration in a cooler until you're ready to use them.

BAKED GOODS

If you have the ability and are comfortable with baking at your tailgate, feel free to prepare any baked goods you wish on-site. However, baking muffins, cakes, and cookies the day before will save you time and provide guests with a delicious treat to eat upon their arrival.

MEATS, MARINADES, AND RUBS

Marinating, assembling, trimming, and brining should be done prior to your arrival at the tailgate. When you're smoking a shoulder or grilling ribs, make sure to pay attention to the specific recipe's instructions about when to apply the rub. If you're bringing rubs and sauces to your tailgate, pack them in a sealable container, ready for use.

PACKING YOUR COOLER

Sealable plastic containers come in a variety of sizes that will stack easily in your cooler. Labeling the contents of each container will prevent confusion when cooking multiple meals. For easier cooking, stack containers in order with the ingredients for the first menu items you'll prepare on top.

To keep your cooler cold, use reusable freezer packs rather than ice. Freezer packs are preferable because they will not fill the cooler with water as they melt. Cooking multiple meals throughout the day? Think about how long some ingredients will need to stay cold. If your tailgate menu is large, you may need separate coolers for each meal.

Tailgating Food Safety

Cooking in a parking lot "kitchen" creates a risk of food poisoning through cross-contamination, food spoilage, and improperly cooked food. Cross-contamination occurs when the bacteria from raw meat comes into contact with other food. Used cutting boards and knives, containers that held raw meat or poultry, tabletops, and unwashed hands are all items that could contaminate the food you're serving. Here are some ways to avoid contaminating your tailgating spread:

▶ Trim and cut raw meat to cooking size before the tailgate. This will reduce exposure to the raw meat.
▶ Transport raw meat in sealable bags. Place these bags into a sealable container. If a bag leaks, the leak will be isolated in the container. At the tailgate, dispose of the bags when you've cooked the meat.
▶ Dedicate one cooler for beverages and one for raw meat and other ingredients. This will do two things. First, it will keep the raw meat away from the bottled beverages. Second, by opening the meat cooler only when you're ready to cook, you'll keep perishable items cooler throughout the day.

Perishable food that sits out at room temperature for more than two hours can lead to bacteria growth and spoilage. To avoid this, keep food at its proper temperature on game day.

▶ When serving perishable foods on a hot game day, keep them stored in a cooler that's below 40° until you're ready to prepare or serve them.

Louisiana State fan Jay Ducote grilling on a custom-built keg grill

► Hot dishes that you're planning on holding throughout the day should be kept above 140°. Keeping them in a slow cooker, over a low burner, or in a chafing dish will keep them warm and prevent bacteria from growing.

► Having a meat thermometer on hand and cooking meat items to internal temperatures of 145° for pork, 160° for burgers, and 165° for poultry will ensure that all your dishes are cooked safely. When you remove cooked items from the grill or smoker, let them rest before serving.

Cooking Equipment

Grills, propane burners, slow cookers, camping ovens, and smokers will allow you to grill, griddle, fry, boil, slow cook, or smoke items at your tailgate. The recipes in this book specify which equipment to use for each dish. Make sure you have enough propane or charcoal to fuel your cooking appliance. Grilling gloves, metal tongs, spatulas, a meat thermometer, a frying thermometer, and a wire spider for deep-frying are important items to have at your tailgate.

Creating a Comfortable Party Environment

Providing your guests with a comfortable space is just as important as leaving them with full stomachs. Here are a few items that will help you create a comfortable tailgating environment for all:

► 10 × 10-foot pop-up tent with walls to block out inclement weather

► Foldable chairs for sitting and socializing

► Space heater to warm the inside of your tent on cold mornings

► TVs and a satellite dish to watch other games as you wait for yours to begin

► Gasoline-powered generator to power TVs and other convenience items

► Rain gear for afternoon storms that may pop up

A Tailgating Box

In your kitchen, you have a "junk drawer." In it are items that might not be used every day but are there when you need them. Try having the same sort of junk drawer for tailgating. Here is a look at what Florida fan Nicole Brockhouse always brings to her tailgate:

> I have a "tailgating box" that contains the essentials. It's a huge Rubbermaid box that never gets unpacked. It's got blue and orange napkins, orange and blue tablecloths, paper plates, plastic cups, utensils (for serving and eating), tons of extra koozies, a bottle opener, fun blue and orange serving platters and bowls, trash bags and paper towels, etc. I found that we were using the same things for every game, so it was easier to just keep them all in that box and throw it in the car. I never have to worry about forgetting anything. Plus, someone always forgets a koozie, so it's nice to have a stash.

Your tailgating box can stay packed all season long. After each game, make sure to replenish items you used up during the tailgate. If you aren't quite sure what to put into your tailgating toolbox, here is a list of frequently forgotten tailgating items:

- ▶ Hand sanitizer and antibacterial wipes—great for dirty hands and cleaning out dirty pots before the ride home.
- ▶ Paper towels—a versatile item that can help you clean up spills or dirty hands and faces. They may also be dabbed with oil to lubricate grill grates. Running a bungee cord through the roll and attaching it to a tent frame makes for easy storage.
- ▶ Can opener—if you have any canned ingredients that may need opening, don't forget one of these.
- ▶ Plastic disposable gloves—used for handling raw meat or tearing apart a cooked pork shoulder. If you know that a task may leave your hands messier than you'd like or you have concerns about cross-contamination, use a pair of disposable gloves.

- ▶ Pot holders and grilling mitts—these will protect your hands and, when placed on a plastic table, can serve as hot pads.
- ▶ Matches—these aren't just for lighting charcoal; if the electric starter on your grill fails, you'll need a way to light the burner.
- ▶ Trash bags—place a trash bag over a collapsible laundry hamper to create a quick and portable trash can.
- ▶ Flashlight—if you have a late-season night game, it may get dark fairly early. A flashlight is a must for finding keys and making sure you have everything packed up.
- ▶ First aid kit—it's always good to be prepared for any potential cuts, scrapes, or injuries that could happen.
- ▶ Sunscreen—it may not seem like you need it, but the next day, you'll be glad you remembered to apply it.
- ▶ Insect spray—depending on your location, mosquitoes may also try to have a bite at your tailgate.

Establishing Your Prep Station

Like cooking at home, cooking on-site requires a prep area. This area can be as small as a side table on your grill. If you need more room, a folding card table may do the trick. Station the area next to your cooking equipment, and use it as a place to add rub to meat, to batter and prepare foods for frying, to let meat rest after cooking, or for any other preparations you may need to make prior to serving food to your guests. Separating this area from the tailgating spread will also help prevent cross-contamination.

The Tailgating Buffet

Are you expecting a large crowd? Do you know that you'll have many guests popping in and out throughout the day? If so, a self-service buffet is the best way to feed your guests on game day. On a folding table or other flat surface, place disposable plates, trays, bowls, utensils, cups, and napkins; next to that, have the sides, main course, and remaining appetizers; place the drinks and desserts on the far end. As the day goes on, simply remove finished dishes to make room for the next items. If you have room for multiple tables, then setting up separate drink and appetizer tables allows you to alleviate any congestion that may be caused by having many people ready to eat at once.

Serving bowls with sealable lids allow for the easy transportation of side dishes and appetizers. The lids will also help prevent bugs from landing on the food.

Beverages can be kept in plastic sealable pitchers or jugs. Having a dedicated bag of ice and an ice scoop for guests to use will always ensure that homemade beverages or cocktails are nice and cold.

A box of pop-up, deli-style waxed paper (like you might find in a self-service bakery section) is perfect for holding cookies, cheese wafers, sandwiches, or a giant turkey leg. These little squares of waxed paper are ideal for snackers who don't want a full plate. Keeping a box on your tailgating table will make it easy for guests to grab a treat without having to commit to a plate.

Dealing with Waste

Always leave your tailgating spot cleaner than you found it. Bring a box of trash bags with you, and make sure you have trash receptacles that guests can use to dispose of their leftovers, plates, cups, and utensils. Placing a trash bag inside of a collapsible laundry hamper makes a convenient and portable trash can. Having two trash cans and marking one for recyclable goods will allow guests to separate their trash from recyclables.

I've seen tailgaters take a "green" approach and dine on reusable plates and use silverware and drinking glasses from their home. If your tailgate is too large for this practice, purchasing recycled disposable products will contribute to a "green" tailgate.

If you're frying at your tailgate, after you're finished with the oil and it has cooled, use a funnel to pour it back into its container.

Due to the lack of refrigeration, leftover perishable food should be given away to nearby tailgaters or thrown away before leaving campus. After sitting out all day, this food may no longer be safe to take home with you, much less to consume later in the week. Having an estimate of the number of guests attending your tailgate will help you plan ahead and avoid wasting food.

Packing Your Team Spirit

Tailgaters take pride in using their creativity to show their team spirit. Throughout my travels, I saw no shortage of ways in which tailgaters were able to add some personal style to their game-day setup. Virginia Tech fan Allison Goin Wash incorporates maroon and orange into her tailgate whenever possible. She told me a little bit about what she brings to show her team spirit on game day: "Our school colors are in everything from food colorings to drinks, plates, napkins, tablecloths, serving dishes, and utensils. This year, I'm really stepping up my tailgating game and making a much more colorful and lively tailgate (battery-operated chandelier for the tent, floor mats/welcome mats, chalkboard with menu, etc.). My favorite tailgating piece has been our maroon Ford F-150 (yes, we would only buy a maroon truck)." Allison went on to tell me that on game days in Blacksburg, "even the trees wake up donning their best maroon and orange."

I've seen thousands of fans who take Allison's approach to team spirit with their tailgating supplies. When you're choosing cups, plates, napkins, and utensils, make the extra effort to find these items in your favorite team's colors. Your tailgating tent, table, and accessories are all ways you can show pride in your team. I've seen tailgaters go as far as having their grills powder-coated in Kentucky blue at an auto body shop.

Many tailgaters throughout the South choose to add a level of sophistication to their game-day spreads. It isn't uncommon to see appetizers served on silver platters or china with prints that incorporate a particular team's colors. Chandeliers hanging from tents, large vases with ornate floral arrangements, and fine linens draped across tiered serving displays are ways tailgaters choose to present their food.

Incorporating your team's colors doesn't end with what you eat or even with what you eat on. Every team has easily attainable pom-poms and koozies in their school colors. Some tailgates will display a larger-than-life inflatable version of their team's mascot. Otherwise, telescoping flagpoles are a popular way to fly your team's colors and show your allegiance.

Auburn fans celebrating at Toomer's Corner after a win over Georgia in 2010

Cornhole, or bag toss, is currently one of the most popular tailgating games. On game day, you'll see foursomes trying to toss beanbags through circular holes in an elevated rectangular board. The object of the game is the same everywhere, but the designs painted on the boards vary greatly. Tailgaters take pride in having custompainted boards. From simple color-blocking patterns to intricate illustrations of a team's mascot, cornhole boards are a way for fans to show school spirit and have fun at the same time.

A few fan bases have unique items that appear at tailgates and aren't usually found on packing lists. At Auburn University, tailgaters always have at least one full roll of toilet paper in their tent. The toilet paper is saved for after the game. When Auburn wins, fans will rush from the stadium to TP the oak trees in Toomer's Corner.

The cowbell is an essential accessory for all Mississippi State fans. The bells are welded to handles and decorated in a variety of maroon and white color combinations. There's no clear under-standing of when fans started to use cowbells, but over the years, fans in Starkville have nevertheless adopted the cowbell as a part of their game-day packing list. They are brought to every tailgate and can be heard ringing throughout the day. Many stadiums outside of Starkville don't allow them inside, but that hasn't deterred Bulldog fans or the cowbell's place in Mississippi State game-day tradition.

Off-Season Testing

The off-season—or, in particular, the summer before tailgating sea-son begins—is the time to figure out how to expand your tailgate. Maybe you want to add a propane burner or a smoker? The off-season is when you should see how this new recipe or cooking technique will work on your equipment and fit into your tailgating style. A tailgate isn't the place to smoke your first pork shoulder. Instead, throw a "homegate" with your neighbors. Testing recipes and techniques in the comfort of your own home will allow you to fine-tune them so that when it's time to perform at the tailgate, you know your meats will be cooked correctly and the flavors will come out perfectly. After all, spending time with your friends in your backyard and testing new tailgating recipes doesn't sound like a bad use of a weekend, does it?

Notes on Products and Procedures

In some of the recipes in this book, you'll see specific brand-name ingredients used, including products such as Tabasco sauce or Bisquick. When you see a specific brand-name ingredient listed, I've chosen that ingredient for its specific flavor qualities and flavor profile. Not all hot sauces are the same. The vast majority of these in-gredients should be available at your grocery store. If for some reason you can't find them, you may use a substitute, but you may affect the seasoning and flavor of the final dish.

A note about baking: I often recommend baking on a lined baking sheet. This means the baking sheet needs to have a nonstick silicone baking mat or a piece of parchment paper lining it. A cake tester can be the blade of a knife or toothpick. When inserted into fully baked goods and removed, it will come out clean.

Drinks

To many fans, game-day beverages are just as important as the food. Some tailgaters have a signature cocktail like the "Purple Stuff" I saw at East Carolina, while others prefer to "drink the competition" with a weekly special inspired by the opposing team. At the Georgia v. Boise State game, a group of Bulldog fans used blue curaçao to make "Smurf-Turf Margaritas" intended to mock Boise State's electric blue field.

Alcoholic beverages are popular at any social gathering, but it's important to pace yourself on game day. Having plenty of water and nonalcoholic options on hand will ensure that your guests will never go thirsty. For the hot early-season games, pack extra water to keep in the cooler. This will help prevent your guests from suffering heat exhaustion and dehydration. In this section, you'll find my favorite beverages to bring to your tailgate.

Oranges-n-Cream Punch

Oranges-n-Cream Punch

Cool, creamy, and orange, this punch packs a punch. It can easily be assembled on-site and can serve a crowd.

MAKES ABOUT 1 GALLON

2 (12-ounce) cans of frozen orange juice concentrate, thawed
2 cups whipped cream–flavored vodka
1 cup heavy whipping cream
⅓ cup orange liqueur
1 (12-ounce) bottle of clear cream soda
2 liters seltzer water
Maraschino cherries for garnish

In a sealable container, add the orange juice concentrate, vodka, whipping cream, and orange liqueur and stir together. Refrigerate overnight and transport in a cooler to your tailgate. At the tailgate, pour the orange and cream mixture into a punch bowl or large pitcher. Add the cream soda and stir. Add the seltzer and stir. Serve over ice and garnish with a cherry.

Lime Cooler Punch

Lime Cooler Punch is family friendly and refreshing, mixes together on-site, and is a nice alternative to soft drinks.

MAKES ABOUT 1 GALLON

2 (12-ounce) cans of frozen limeade concentrate, thawed
1 cup pineapple juice
¼ cup fresh lime juice
3 liters seltzer water
2 limes

In a sealable container, add the limeade concentrate, pineapple juice, and lime juice. Stir together until mixed. Refrigerate overnight. At the tailgate, pour the limeade mixture into a large serving container. Add the seltzer water and stir. Slice the limes into thin slices, add to the punch, and stir. Serve over ice.

Raspberry Lemonade

Homemade lemonade requires a little bit of elbow grease, but the results are worth it. The clean, bright flavors of raspberry and lemon will quench your thirst on the hottest of game days.

MAKES ABOUT ¾ GALLON

3 cups sugar
2 cups water
1½ cups frozen raspberries
Zest from 2 lemons
Pinch of salt
3 cups fresh lemon juice
5 cups water
Raspberries and lemon slices for garnish

To make the raspberry base, add the sugar, water, raspberries, lemon zest, and salt to a medium-sized saucepan. Bring to a boil while stirring occasionally. Reduce to a simmer and let simmer for 10 minutes, stirring occasionally. Remove from heat and let cool for 10 minutes. Pour the syrup through a fine mesh strainer.

In a gallon-sized container, add the lemon juice, water, and raspberry syrup. Stir. Refrigerate overnight and transport in a sealable pitcher to your tailgate. Serve over ice and garnish with fresh raspberries and a lemon slice.

Razzle Dazzle Cocktail

It's fun to have your guests guess what's in this game-day cocktail. The Razzle Dazzle may confuse them, but they'll all agree it tastes great.

MAKES 1 DRINK

1 cup Raspberry Lemonade (page 16)
1½ ounces Pink Bubblegum Vodka (page 27)
½ ounce cherry-flavored vodka
1 teaspoon maraschino cherry juice
1 teaspoon fresh lime juice
Maraschino cherry for garnish

In either a cocktail shaker or a cup, add all the ingredients. Shake or stir until evenly mixed. Serve over the ice and garnish with a maraschino cherry.

Sweet Iced Tea

In the South, there's an unwritten rule: every social event has sweet iced tea. Since tailgates are the social events of the fall, your guests will appreciate having sweet tea on hand. This is how I like to drink my tea, but feel free to adjust the amount of sugar to taste.

MAKES 1 GALLON

8 cups boiling water
4 family-sized iced tea bags
1½ cups sugar
8 cups cold water

In a large pot, bring the water to a boil. Add the tea bags and turn off heat. Allow the bags to steep for 3 minutes. Remove the tea bags with a spoon. Add the sugar and stir until dissolved. Pour into a gallon-sized serving container. Add the cold water and stir. Let cool and refrigerate overnight. Serve over ice.

Game-Day Greetings

Game days in the South have their own dialect, filled with phrases, gestures, cheers, and songs unique to each fan base.

In Tuscaloosa, fans greet each other by saying "Roll Tide!" On the other side of the state, Auburn fans welcome one another with "War Eagle!" Like "Aloha," these phrases work as greetings, good-byes, and complete sentences. Be careful, though. If you say "Roll Tide!" to an Auburn fan, it's considered an insult.

Some fan bases have special phrases for visiting teams. If you're visiting the "Swamp" in Gainesville, don't be surprised if, on your way to the game, you're called "Gator bait" by Florida fans. Auburn and Louisiana State each have a tiger as mascot, and it's not uncommon to hear fans calling the opposing team's visiting fans "Tiger bait." Often these taunts will be accompanied by hand gestures. In Tallahassee, Florida State fans make a chopping motion, representing a tomahawk, as they shout a war chant. In Gainesville, Gator fans fully extend their arms, touch their palms, and then lift the top arm up and down to mimic the motion of an alligator's jaws.

In Fayetteville, Arkansas, fans gather with their chant dubbed Calling the Hogs. The hog call begins with raising your arm and letting out an extended "Wooooooooooo!" followed by a fist pump while chanting, "Pig! Sooie!" This is repeated two more times and concludes with an energetic "Razorbacks!"

Hand signals aren't just for intimidating an opponent; they also are used as a way to show solidarity and to salute fellow fans. At the University of Miami, fans use two hands to create a "U" symbolizing their nickname, "The U."

In the Lone Star State, every team uses a hand gesture as a way for fans to silently show camaraderie: Texas Tech's "Guns Up" can be seen in Lubbock; Houston fans will show their "Cougar Paw," while the Baylor fans have their "Bear Claw"; Texas Christian and Southern Methodist have similar two-fingered gestures referred to as the "Horned Frog" and "Pony Ears," respectively; Texas A&M's single thumb in the air is referred to as "Gig 'em." At the University of North Texas and Texas State University, the "Eagle Claw" and "Heart of Texas State" hand signs can be seen on game days or whenever team spirit is called for.

The University of Texas's "Hook 'em Horns" is a gesture inspired by the horns of the school's mascot, Bevo. This gesture is formed by folding down your thumb, middle, and ring fingers, then extending your pointer and pinky fingers outward to resemble the horns of a steer. Seen everywhere the Longhorns play, this hand gesture has become so popular that Texas's rival to the north has adopted it. The University of Oklahoma's version has one slight difference: the horns are turned upside down. When Oklahoma and Texas fans gather every year in Dallas, the "Hook 'em" sign can be seen everywhere, pointing both up and down, depending on what team is being supported.

You'll see hand gestures in South Carolina, where Gamecock fans make a "Spur" with their hands by extending their thumb and pinky finger. North Carolina State fans' "Wolf Pack" and the University of South Florida's "Go Bulls" are similar to the Texas "Hook 'em." Each school has its own variation. In Nashville, the Vanderbilt Commodores create a VU hand signal using their thumb and index and middle fingers.

Songs are another way for fans to express their team spirit. There's no better way to show solidarity than to have hundreds or thousands of people singing in unison. Every school has a fight song, but some fan bases have adopted popular, commercially successful songs as a part of their game-day tradition. John Denver's "Country Roads" is played at every Mountaineer football game. West Virginia fans have incorporated it into their pregame festivities; I heard it repeatedly in the Blue Lot outside Milan Puskar Stadium. Upon hearing the first notes, swarms of Mountaineer fans gather around and sing until the end. Felice and Boudleaux Bryant's "Rocky Top" is a tune you either love or hate. In Knoxville, Tennessee, fans sing along from the first banjo note all the way until the last words, "Rocky Top, Tennessee." Visiting teams cover their ears and roll their eyes when they hear the song begin.

Some fan bases prefer simple chants—a few rhythmic sentences—for showing their enthusiasm. While I was in Oxford, Mississippi, for a matchup between Ole Miss and the University of Texas, the Grove was filled with each fan base's signature chant. On the Ole Miss side, when someone yelled, "Are you ready?," the Grove erupted in a response of

Hell yeah! Damn right!
Hotty Toddy, gosh almighty,
Who the hell are we? Hey!
Flim flam, bim bam
Ole Miss by damn!

On the Texas side, when a group yelled, "Texas!," the response would be "Fight!" followed by the first group chanting "Texas!" and the second group answering again with "Fight!" This spontaneous cheering occurred more frequently as kickoff approached.

For Texas A&M fans in College Station, game-

Texas A&M fans during the Midnight Yell

day chants and cheers are practiced with military precision. The night before home games, students and fans of all ages will gather together inside Kyle Field for the Midnight Yell. Over 25,000 fans will assemble for this one-of-a-kind midnight pep rally. Cheerleaders, known as Yell Leaders, tell stories about Aggies from the past, tell jokes about the opposition, and sing fight songs and cheers. Most important, Yell Leaders will run through all the cheers and "pass backs" that will cue the cheers to be used in the game the following day. When walking away from the Midnight Yell, you may find it hard to fall asleep. Luckily, kickoff is only a few hours away. ∎

White or Red Sangria

Sangria in a plastic wine glass is a great way to relax and cool down on a warm game day. Serving the sangria in a wide-mouth container with a ladle makes it easy for guests to have both wine and fruit in their glass. Leaving the fruit in the sangria mix overnight will cause the fruit to soak up a fair amount of alcohol. Eating this fruit may cause you to consume more alcohol than you planned!

MAKES 8 SERVINGS

White Sangria
2 bottles of your favorite white wine
1/4 cup orange blossom honey or 1/3 cup simple syrup (see note)
1/2 cup orange liqueur
1 pint fresh raspberries
4 cups fresh pineapple chunks (about 1 1/2 pounds), cut into bite-sized pieces
3 plums, 2 nectarines, or 1 large Gala apple, cut into bite-sized pieces
1 lemon, thinly sliced into rounds and seeded

Red Sangria
2 bottles of your favorite red wine
1/3 cup simple syrup (see note)
1/2 cup orange liqueur
1 pint blackberries
1 pint raspberries
2 large navel oranges, thinly sliced and quartered
1 lime, thinly sliced

In a gallon pitcher, combine the wine, honey or simple syrup, and liqueur. Stir well. Add the fruit to the wine mixture and stir. If using an apple, toss the apple pieces in 1 teaspoon of lemon juice before adding to the sangria. Seal the pitcher and refrigerate overnight.

Note: For 1 1/2 cups of syrup, add 1 cup sugar and 1 cup water to a small saucepan and bring to a boil. Reduce to a simmer and stir until all the sugar has dissolved. Remove from heat. The syrup can be used immediately or refrigerated for 2–3 weeks.

White Sangria

Mimosa Trio

If you see a carton of orange juice at a tailgate, it usually means there's a champagne bottle not too far away. I start my Mimosa Trio with a traditional mimosa. Mary Mitchell Hartnett likes to take her mimosa one step further. She begins all her Florida game days with a special concoction, complete with its own song and dance. Her simple combination of orange juice, champagne, and vodka is called a Shazam. She swears it's not a game day unless she's had one. If you don't care for champagne, try substituting beer. Beer and orange juice may sound strange, but make a Beermosa once, and you'll be convinced. If you're looking for a fun way to serve your morning mimosas, try plastic champagne flutes.

MAKES 1 DRINK

Traditional Mimosa
1 part orange juice
1 part champagne

Shazam
1 part orange juice
1 part champagne
1 shot of vodka

Beermosa
1 part pilsner or pale ale
1 part orange juice

Pour the ingredients for each drink into a plastic cup and stir.

Traditional Mimosa

Bloody Mary Bar

The tailgater's relationship with a Bloody Mary is one with no middle ground. It's either your go-to pregame drink, or you don't understand how someone could drink something with a salad coming out of it. Regardless of your opinion, there are sure to be guests at your tailgate who will love you when they see a self-serve Bloody Mary Bar set up. The basic bar includes Bloody Mary mix, vodka or jalapeño pepper vodka, and ice. There are an infinite number of garnishes you can top a Bloody Mary with. Some guests will be fine with just a celery stalk, while others will load theirs up with home-made quick-pickled carrots, beans, onions, radishes, cocktail onions, olives, shrimp, lemon slices, and extra hot sauce. Prepare the mix ahead of time and serve with ice in cups with a salted rim.

MAKES 8 SERVINGS

Bloody Mary Mix
1 (46-ounce) bottle of tomato juice
2 tablespoons lime juice
4 teaspoons Worcestershire sauce
1 tablespoon prepared horseradish
1 teaspoon celery salt
¼ teaspoon McCormick Coarse Ground Black Pepper
1 teaspoon Tabasco sauce

Assorted garnishes and vodkas

In a large plastic pitcher, combine all the ingredients for the mix and stir until thoroughly blended. Refrigerate overnight and transport in a cooler to the tailgate.

At the tailgate, set up your bar with the Bloody Mary mix and an assortment of toppings, cups, ice, and vodkas. Allow guests to make versions that are tailored to their specific tastes.

Bloody Mary

Archie's Fred

A family friend who is a huge Georgetown Hoya fan introduced me to this rum drink. Here's how I've been drinking it ever since.

MAKES 1 DRINK

1 cup pineapple juice
2 ounces Myers's Original Dark Rum
1 tablespoon fresh lime juice
Lime slice for garnish

In either a cocktail shaker or a cup, add all the ingredients. Shake or stir until evenly mixed. Serve over the ice and garnish with a lime slice.

Blueberry Moon Cocktail

The Blueberry Moon is an invigorating combination of blueberry, lime, ginger, and cherry flavors that folks are sure to enjoy. The blueberry syrup and the lime juice should be prepared the night before and the final drink assembled on-site.

MAKES ABOUT 1 GALLON

1 pound frozen blueberries
2 cups sugar
1 1/2 cups moonshine
1 cup fresh lime juice
1/2 cup cherry-flavored vodka
2 liters ginger ale
2 limes, thinly sliced
Additional lime slices for garnish

Place the blueberries and sugar in a medium-sized saucepan. Heat on low, stirring occasionally, until the blueberries thaw and the sugar has dissolved. Increase heat to medium and bring to a simmer. Let simmer for 5 minutes, stirring occasionally. Press the syrup through a fine mesh strainer, releasing any remaining blueberry juice. Use the syrup immediately or store covered in the refrigerator for a week.

Blueberry Moon Cocktail

To assemble this beverage on-site, add the blueberry syrup, moonshine, lime juice, and vodka to a gallon pitcher and stir. Add the ginger ale and stir. Add the sliced limes and stir. Serve over ice and garnish with a lime slice.

Bacon Whiskey

If you're in town for a Vanderbilt game, don't miss the Patterson House in Nashville, Tennessee. It isn't your typical bar. The walls of this restored house are lined with bookcases and ornate wallpaper. It's sitting room only. You aren't allowed to stand at the bar and wait for a drink; you must wait for a seat to open up before you may enter. On the drink menu is something called a Bacon Old-Fashioned. The bartender told me the bacon-infused spirit is made through a process called "fat washing" in which liquid fat is poured into alcohol, shaken, and left to infuse for a period of time. The mixture is then frozen, which separates the fat so the infused liquor can be drained off. As a bacon lover, I had to order it. Sure enough, I could taste the bacon.

MAKES ABOUT 2½ CUPS

½ cup warm bacon drippings, rendered from 8–10 slices of cooked premium bacon
2½ cups premium whiskey or bourbon

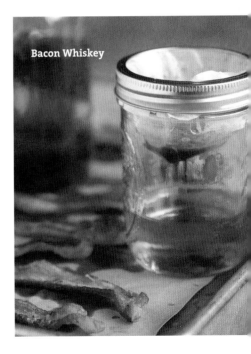

Bacon Whiskey

Fold a paper coffee filter over a wide-mouth Mason jar. Screw on the jar's ring to secure the coffee filter. Pour the warm bacon drippings through the coffee filter, straining out any pieces of bacon.

Add the filtered drippings and whiskey to a sealable container. Seal the container, then give it a few shakes and let the mixture infuse for 3–4 hours. Store the container in the freezer overnight. The next morning, you'll find that the fat has separated and solidified. Remove any large pieces of frozen bacon fat with a spoon. Run the bacon whiskey through a fine mesh screen or coffee filter to remove any smaller solidified pieces of fat. Use as a substitute for whiskey or bourbon in any cocktail.

Infused Vodka Trio

Creating infused liquors will give your tailgating cocktails a unique taste. Infusion works by placing an infusing agent (a fruit, vegetable, or spice) into a spirit and letting the mixture sit for a period of time. The best-tasting infused spirits use good-quality alcohol and high-quality infusing agents. Here are three of my favorite vodka infusions.

MAKES ABOUT 2 CUPS

Lemon-Lime Vodka
4 lemons
4 limes
$\frac{1}{2}$ liter good-quality vodka

Wash and thoroughly clean the lemons and limes. Using a sharp knife or vegetable peeler, remove the citrus skin. Take care to leave as much of the bitter-tasting white pith on the fruit as possible. Place the skins in a large sealable container and add the vodka. Seal the container. Let the mixture soak for 2 days. Shake twice a day. The vodka will turn a bright yellow-green color. Pour the vodka through a coffee filter to remove all the pieces of lemon and lime. For a refreshing change of taste, use in your next vodka tonic.

Jalapeño Pepper Vodka
2–4 jalapeño peppers
1$\frac{1}{2}$ teaspoons whole peppercorns
$\frac{1}{2}$ liter good-quality vodka

Wash the jalapeños. Cut 4 slits, one on each side, in each pepper. Place the peppers and peppercorns in a large sealable container and add the vodka. Seal the container. Let the mixture infuse for three days. Shake twice a day. The liquid will turn darker in color. Pour the vodka through a coffee filter to remove the jalapeños and peppercorns. For guests who like a little bit of heat in their drink, this is a great addition to your next Bloody Mary Bar (page 22).

Pink Bubblegum Vodka

15 pieces of pink bubble gum (I use Dubble Bubble)
½ liter good-quality vodka

Unwrap the bubble gum pieces and place them in a large sealable container. Pour in the vodka, making sure to cover the bubble gum. Seal the container. This infusion will happen quickly. Let the mixture infuse for 4–6 hours, shaking every hour. The liquid will turn bright pink. Pour the vodka through a coffee filter to remove all pieces of gum.

Lemon Bar Shots

Reminiscent of the classic lemon bar cookie, lemon bar Jell-O shots are a fun way to drink your dessert. Prepare them the night before and dust with confectioners' sugar before serving.

MAKES 8 SERVINGS

2 (3-ounce) boxes of lemon Jell-O
2 cups boiling water
9 tablespoons cold water
1 cup cake-flavored vodka
¼ cup heavy whipping cream
1 tablespoon Amaretto
2 teaspoons grated lemon zest
Confectioners' sugar for garnish

Add the Jell-O to a medium-sized bowl. Pour in the boiling water and stir until the gelatin has completely dissolved. Add the cold water, vodka, whipping cream, Amaretto, and lemon zest and stir. Pour into an 8 × 8-inch metal cake pan. Refrigerate uncovered overnight. Cut into squares and dust with confectioners' sugar right before serving.

Lemon Bar Shots

Southern Game-Day Attire

You have your colored plates and colored tablecloth, and you've even color-coded your menu. Your tailgate is team-themed, and the loyalty you show can't be questioned. The final thing you need is an outfit based on your team's colors.

How you do this is completely up to you and your style. I've seen everything from full seersucker suits in Oxford, Mississippi, to fans covered in gold and blue body paint at West Virginia. Some fans wear spandex suits that cover their bodies from head to toe in one color. People often wear the jerseys of their favorite players. To accessorize, women adorn themselves with a variety of colored necklaces, earrings, and hair accessories in their team's colors. Those who are behind grills or are preparing food will protect their outfits with aprons and their hands with oven mitts in their team's colors.

While jerseys, polo shirts, T-shirts, and jeans are all commonplace, in the South, many fans take a more formal approach to their game-day attire.

Formal Tailgating Wear

To Auburn fan Rachel Caudle, "game day is like going to church on Sunday—you have to be at your best!" She is not alone in her view of game-day attire. Women of all ages agree that early-season games are the perfect time to wear lightweight, knee-length sundresses. From campus to campus, color and cut will vary. At UNC, they wear Carolina blue and white; at Georgia, a combination of red, black, and white; and in Norman, Oklahoma, crimson and cream.

With the women at tailgates dressed to impress, many gentlemen take note. Across the South, you'll see men wearing button-down shirts with ties or bow ties and even suits at pregame tailgates. I can assure you that this kind of game-day attire appears nowhere else in the country. Many men wear pants embroidered with their team's logo or in their school colors. I've seen a Tennessee fan with a white suit and orange button-down shirt and Georgia fans with full red seersucker suits and bow ties; at Ole Miss, a blue seersucker jacket with a red and blue bow tie is common. As the season progresses and weather gets cooler, fans will find other ways to dress their best. Women wear peacoats in their team's colors, while men wear sweaters over their ties and button-down shirts.

Game-Day Prints

For some schools, color is not a strong enough way to show school spirit; a print is needed. Here are two of the most popular prints for game day.

ALABAMA HOUNDSTOOTH

The late Paul "Bear" Bryant was a legendary football coach at Alabama. His six national championships make him one of the greatest college football coaches of all time. Alabama's football stadium bears his name and his statue stands guard out front, so "the Bear's" presence is always felt on game day.

During his coaching career, Coach Bryant was routinely seen on the sidelines wearing his signature houndstooth hat. Alabama fans have remembered their great coach further by adopting his signature print. They wear houndstooth in any and all forms to show their love and respect for Coach Bryant. From rain boots and shorts to peacoats, hats, scarves, and gloves, on game day every Alabama fan has some accessory or cloth-

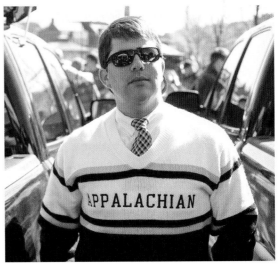

ing item with the houndstooth print on it. While Alabama's school colors are crimson and white, black and white houndstooth is seen wherever Alabama fans tailgate.

TENNESSEE'S CHECKERBOARD

Inside Neyland Stadium, over 100,000 fans cheer the Volunteers on Saturdays. With every possession, the Vols try to take the ball over

the goal line and into their orange and white checkerboard end zone. Fans show their love for the school's end zones in their pregame activities. Thousands of Tennessee fans outside the stadium find a way to incorporate the Vols' signature checkerboard pattern in their festivities, from the way their cornhole boards are painted to the patterns on their tablecloths, pants, and shirts. ∎

Above, clockwise from top left: **Fans at Ole Miss, Tennessee, Appalachian State, and Alabama showing what they wear on game day**

Hot Cocoa with Peppermint Whipped Cream

On cold game days, I never turn down a warm mug of hot cocoa. When it's topped with freshly whipped peppermint-flavored whipped cream, it's a treat that every one of your tailgating neighbors will want.

MAKES 24 SERVINGS

Hot Cocoa Mix (makes 3 cups)
1½ cups granulated sugar
¾ cup cocoa powder
¾ cup confectioners' sugar
1 teaspoon salt

Peppermint Whipped Cream
Pinch of salt
½ cup confectioners' sugar
1 pint heavy whipping cream, chilled
½ teaspoon vanilla extract
½ teaspoon peppermint extract
12 peppermint candies, crushed into a coarse powder

Hot Cocoa
½ cup whole milk per serving
½ cup half-and-half per serving
3 tablespoons hot cocoa mix per serving

Make the hot cocoa mix prior to the tailgate. Add the mix ingredients to the bowl of a food processor and process until thoroughly blended. Store in an airtight, sealable container. Bring the mix and a tablespoon with you to the tailgate.

For the whipped cream, pack the salt and confectioners' sugar in a sealable plastic bag. Premix the whipping cream, vanilla extract, and peppermint extract in a separate container and refrigerate overnight. Pack the crushed peppermint candies in a sealable bag. Transport the cream mix in a cooler to the tailgate. Bring a metal bowl and whisk to the tailgate.

When you're ready for the cocoa, make the whipped cream first. Combine the sugar mixture and cream mixture in a metal bowl. Whisk in a circular motion until the cream forms soft peaks. Add the crushed candies and fold in to incorporate.

To make a serving of hot cocoa, bring the milk and half-and-half to just below a simmer. Remove from heat and stir. In a mug or heat-proof cup, add the dry cocoa mix. Add 1/3 cup of the milk mixture and stir to dissolve the cocoa mix. Add the remaining 2/3 cup of the milk mixture and stir together. Top with a dollop or two of Peppermint Whipped Cream.

Hot Cocoa with Peppermint Whipped Cream

Spiced Hot Cider

When visitors drop by on a chilly game day, offering a mug of this Spiced Hot Cider is something tailgaters of all ages can enjoy. The cider is easy to prepare on-site and can be kept warm all day.

MAKES ABOUT 1 GALLON

1 cup fresh orange juice
$\frac{2}{3}$ cup dark brown sugar
$\frac{1}{4}$ cup fresh lemon juice
2 tablespoons honey
$\frac{1}{4}$ teaspoon salt
5 cinnamon sticks
1 tablespoon whole cloves
1 teaspoon whole allspice
1 family-sized iced tea bag
1 gallon apple cider
Orange slices for garnish

Pour orange juice, dark brown sugar, lemon juice, honey, and salt into a sealable container and refrigerate overnight.

Assemble the spice packet by placing the cinnamon sticks, cloves, allspice, and tea bag onto a sheet of cheesecloth. Gather the cloth around the spices, and tie the top of the packet with cooking twine.

At the tailgate, pour the gallon of cider into a large stockpot and add the orange juice mixture. Bring to a simmer over a propane burner. Add the spice packet and let simmer for 15 minutes, stirring occasionally. Remove the spice packet and reduce heat to low. Keep the cider warm until served. Garnish with an orange slice.

If you'll be on campus game-day morning, I recommend offering your guests something for breakfast. It can be as simple as a basket of muffins and a cup of coffee or as elaborate as a full buffet spread. Whether you treat breakfast as a warm-up, the main event, or something in between, you'll find something here to start your game day off right.

Breakfast

Doughnut French Toast with Raspberry Syrup

Doughnut French Toast with Raspberry Syrup

French toast is usually day-old bread battered in an egg wash and then pan fried until golden brown. To celebrate game day, I prefer a sweeter version. Inspired by Wake Forest fans, I like to make Doughnut French Toast. Winston-Salem, North Carolina, is home to Wake Forest University and is the birthplace of Krispy Kreme Doughnuts. When sliced in half, dunked in an egg wash, and cooked until golden brown, this hot, sweet, and sticky doughnut is the best French toast you could imagine!

MAKES 6 SERVINGS

Doughnut French Toast
½ dozen day-old Krispy Kreme glazed doughnuts
½ cup half-and-half
½ cup 2 percent milk
2 eggs, beaten
1 teaspoon vanilla extract
1 teaspoon confectioners' sugar
Pinch of salt

Raspberry Syrup
1 pound frozen raspberries, thawed
2 cups sugar
1 tablespoon lemon juice
Pinch of salt
2 tablespoons unsalted butter

The night before the tailgate, cut the doughnuts in half, creating 12 discs. Store in a sealed, airtight bag. Add the half-and-half, milk, eggs, vanilla extract, confectioners' sugar, and salt to a sealable container. Store in the refrigerator overnight.

To make the Raspberry Syrup, add the berries, sugar, lemon juice, and salt to a medium-sized pot. Heat over low, stirring occasionally until the berries have thawed and the sugar has dissolved. Increase heat to medium and simmer, stirring frequently, for 10 minutes.

Remove from heat. Run the syrup through a fine mesh strainer to remove all large pieces of berry and the seeds. Add the butter and stir until the syrup and butter are blended. Let cool and transfer to a plastic squeeze bottle.

At the tailgate, stir the egg and milk mixture. Grease a pan or griddle with butter or nonstick cooking spray and place over a burner on medium heat. Place the doughnut halves in the egg-wash mixture, cut-side down. Soak the doughnuts in the mixture for a few seconds. Turn them over and lightly wet the other side. Place each doughnut half, cut-side down, on the hot cooking surface. Cook for a minute or two until light brown. Using a spatula, flip it and briefly cook the other side. Serve with Raspberry Syrup.

Fluffy Sour Cream Pancakes with Blackberry Syrup

In Blacksburg, a group of Virginia Tech fans cooked pancakes on a griddle over a charcoal grill. In Jacksonville, for the Florida v. Georgia game, a Bulldogs fan placed sausage in the middle of a pancake to make a breakfast pig-in-a-blanket. Pancakes are made for tailgating. Their light and fluffy texture is easily cut with a fork and will satisfy even the largest of appetites.

MAKES 4 SERVINGS

Pancakes
1½ cups all-purpose flour
3 tablespoons sugar
1 teaspoon baking soda
1 teaspoon baking powder
¼ teaspoon salt
Pinch of freshly grated nutmeg
½ cup half-and-half
¼ cup 2 percent milk
2 eggs, lightly beaten
1 cup sour cream
1 teaspoon lemon juice

Blackberry Syrup

1 pound frozen blackberries, thawed

2 cups sugar

1 tablespoon lemon juice

Pinch of salt

2 tablespoons unsalted butter

The night before the tailgate, measure out the flour, sugar, baking soda, baking powder, salt, and nutmeg and pack in a sealable container. Measure out the half-and-half, milk, eggs, sour cream, and lemon juice and place in a large sealable container (this will be your mixing bowl at the tailgate). Refrigerate overnight and transport in a cooler to your tailgate.

To make the Blackberry Syrup, add the berries, sugar, lemon juice, and salt to a medium-sized pot. Heat over low, stirring occasionally until the berries have thawed and the sugar has dissolved. Increase heat to medium and simmer, stirring frequently, for 10 minutes.

Remove from heat. Run the syrup through a fine mesh strainer, removing all large pieces of berry and the seeds. Add the butter and stir until it has dissolved. Let cool and transfer to a plastic squeeze bottle.

At your tailgate, pour the flour mixture into the milk and egg mixture and stir until a thick batter forms. It's alright if there are a few lumps in the batter.

Heat a nonstick griddle or nonstick frying pan over a medium-high grill. Cooking temperatures will vary, depending on the distance between your grill's heating element and the pan. If the pancakes cook too quickly, turn down the heat. Using a ¼-cup measuring scoop, drop the batter onto the hot griddling surface. This is a thick batter; you may need to use the back of the measuring cup to spread the batter out in an even layer. Cook until the edges have drawn back and bubbles on the surface begin to pop. Flip and cook the other side. Serve with Blackberry Syrup.

Cinnamon Toast Breakfast Cake with Icing Drizzle

This breakfast cake is delicious. It combines coffee cake, cinnamon toast, and a creamy icing drizzle. A piece of this and a cup of coffee are a great way to welcome your guests to a long day of tailgating.

MAKES 12 SERVINGS

Topping
1 cup granulated sugar
$\frac{1}{2}$ cup all-purpose flour
2 tablespoons ground cinnamon
$\frac{1}{4}$ teaspoon salt
1 stick unsalted butter, melted

Cake
2$\frac{1}{3}$ cups all-purpose flour
2 teaspoons baking powder
1 teaspoon baking soda
$\frac{1}{4}$ teaspoon salt
3 large eggs
1$\frac{1}{2}$ cups granulated sugar
1 cup sour cream
2 teaspoons vanilla extract
1 teaspoon almond extract
2 sticks unsalted butter, melted

Icing Drizzle
1 cup confectioners' sugar
2 tablespoons unsalted butter, softened
2 ounces cream cheese, softened
Pinch of salt
$\frac{1}{4}$ cup heavy whipping cream

Preheat the oven to 350°.

To make the topping, mix together the sugar, flour, cinnamon, and salt in a medium-sized bowl. Pour in the melted butter, stir until blended, and set aside.

To make the cake, mix together the flour, baking powder, baking soda, and salt in a large bowl. In a medium-sized bowl, mix together the eggs, sugar, sour cream, vanilla extract, and almond extract. Add the melted butter and stir.

Pour the egg and butter mixture into the flour mixture. Stir until just blended. Pour the batter into a buttered and floured 9 × 13-inch metal pan. With a fork, stir the cinnamon toast topping until it forms crumbles. Cover the top of the cake with an even layer of the topping. Swirl the topping with a table knife into the batter, making S shapes.

Bake for 25–30 minutes, until an inserted cake tester comes out clean. Let cool.

To make the icing drizzle, place the confectioners' sugar, butter, cream cheese, and salt in a small bowl. Stir with a spoon until well blended, making a thick paste. While stirring, gradually pour in the whipping cream until an icing forms. With the tines of a fork, drizzle the icing over the top of the cooled cake. Since the drizzle remains sticky, use an elevated cake cover in storage and transport.

Sunshine Muffins

Filled with apricots and dates, this fruity combination is a welcome start to any morning. When served with mimosas (page 21), they make for a quick and light breakfast whenever early guests stop by.

MAKES 16 LARGE MUFFINS

1¼ cups whole milk
1 cup grated carrots
2¼ cups all-purpose flour
1 cup sugar
1 tablespoon baking powder
½ teaspoon salt
⅛ teaspoon ground cloves
1 cup chopped dates
½ cup diced dried apricots
2 large eggs, beaten
1 stick unsalted butter, melted
2 teaspoons vanilla extract
½ teaspoon almond extract

Preheat the oven to 350°.

In a large bowl, add the milk and carrots. Let soak for 10 minutes. While the carrots are soaking, measure the flour, sugar, baking powder, salt, and cloves into a large bowl. Stir until the ingredients are evenly incorporated.

Add the dates, apricots, eggs, butter, vanilla extract, and almond extracts to the soaked carrots and milk.

Pour the carrot and milk mixture into the flour mixture. Lightly stir until just blended and a batter forms.

Spoon the batter into a nonstick muffin pan lined with paper muffin cups. Bake for 20–25 minutes. The muffins are done when a tester comes out clean. Remove from the oven, cool in the pan for a few minutes, then remove the muffins from the pan and let cool completely. Store in an airtight sealable container.

Sunshine Muffins and
Bacon and Brown Sugar Muffins
with Bourbon Glaze (p. 42)

Bacon and Brown Sugar Muffins with Bourbon Glaze

Can you have your cake and eat your bacon, too? Yes, you can! This may look like a cupcake, but this breakfast muffin is loaded with bacon and bourbon flavor, perfect for those tailgaters who believe in the power of the pig. When Arkansas is the opponent, this is a must on your "eat the competition" menu.

MAKES 12 LARGE MUFFINS

Muffins

6 slices thick-cut bacon, cooked, drained, and crumbled

1/2 cup dark brown sugar

1/2 cup granulated sugar

2 1/4 cups all-purpose flour

1 tablespoon baking powder

1/2 teaspoon salt

2 large eggs

1 1/4 cups whole milk

1 teaspoon vanilla extract

1 teaspoon bourbon

8 tablespoons unsalted butter, melted

Bourbon Glaze

2 tablespoons unsalted butter, softened

2 tablespoons cream cheese, softened

1 teaspoon bacon drippings, room-temperature

1 cup confectioners' sugar

1 tablespoon dark brown sugar

Pinch of salt

2 tablespoons bourbon

1/2 teaspoon vanilla extract

Preheat the oven to 350°.

Put the bacon and sugars in the bowl of a food processor. Pulse the mixture until the bacon is incorporated into the sugars and resembles coarse meal. Set aside.

In a large mixing bowl, stir together the flour, baking powder, and salt. Add the bacon and sugar mixture. Stir to incorporate and set aside.

In a separate bowl, stir the eggs with a fork to blend. Add the milk, vanilla extract, bourbon, and melted butter and stir. Add the egg and milk mixture to the flour, sugar, and bacon mixture. Stir with a fork until the ingredients are just blended and form a batter.

Spoon the batter into a nonstick muffin pan lined with paper muffin cups. Bake for 20–25 minutes. The muffins are done when a tester comes out clean. Remove from the oven, cool in the pan for a few minutes, then remove the muffins from the pan and let cool completely.

While the muffins are baking, prepare the Bourbon Glaze. Put the butter, cream cheese, and bacon drippings into a medium bowl and stir until blended. Add the sugars and salt; stir until well blended. Add the bourbon and vanilla extract and stir until a smooth glaze forms.

Dip the cooled muffin tops into the Bourbon Glaze, and let the muffins sit at room temperature until the glaze is set. Store in an airtight container.

Blueberry Muffins with Blackberry Butter

Everyone loves a delicious blueberry muffin. This one won't disappoint. When Blackberry Butter is added, you have a treat ready for your tailgating breakfast spread.

MAKES 12 MUFFINS

Muffins

2 cups all-purpose flour

¾ cup sugar

2 tablespoons plain white cornmeal

1 tablespoon baking powder

½ teaspoon salt

1 cup blueberries

1¼ cups whole milk

2 large eggs, beaten

1 stick unsalted butter, melted

1 teaspoon vanilla extract

¼ teaspoon almond extract

Blackberry Butter

6 tablespoons unsalted butter, softened

6 tablespoons seedless blackberry jam

¼ teaspoon grated lemon zest

⅛ teaspoon ground cloves

Pinch of salt

Preheat the oven to 350°.

In a large bowl, add the flour, sugar, cornmeal, baking powder, and salt. Mix together until evenly distributed. Add the blueberries and lightly toss.

In a medium-sized bowl, add the milk, eggs, butter, vanilla extract, and almond extract. Stir together until evenly incorporated.

Pour the milk mixture into the flour mixture. Lightly stir together until just blended and a batter forms.

Spoon the batter into a nonstick muffin pan lined with paper muffin cups. Bake for 20–25 minutes. The muffins are done when a tester comes out clean. Remove from the oven, cool in the pan for a few minutes, then remove the muffins from the pan and let cool completely. Store in a sealable container overnight.

To make the blackberry butter, add the butter, jam, lemon zest, cloves, and salt to the bowl of a food processor. Process until the butter and jam are well blended. Remove from the processor and place in a serving container, such as a sealable glass bowl or ramekin. Refrigerate overnight before using. Transport in a cooler to your tailgate and set out upon arrival.

Unique Tailgating Transportation

No matter where you're spending your game day, every tailgater has one thing that he or she must do: get to the game. Travel by car is by far the most common way, but many tailgaters have found other solutions.

The RV

For tailgaters who live far away and want to make their tailgating experience last for more than just a weekend, the RV is the best way to travel. When tailgating by RV, you bring all the comforts of home with you. These comforts include a kitchen, bedroom, and bathroom. Purchasing a vehicle of this size shows you're committed to traveling with your team wherever it goes. At schools across the South, many RV owners arrive on Thursday or even Wednesday for a Saturday game. And because they have all the comforts of home at their disposal, these tailgaters host very large and impressive tailgating celebrations that begin well before game day.

Custom Tailgating Vehicles

Many tailgaters show their team spirit and athletic allegiances by decorating and customizing their cars. In the lots surrounding stadiums, I've seen everything from an orange and blue van adorned with a stuffed tiger on top in Auburn to a blue hearse with a giant wasp decal on the side in Emory, Virginia. Some fans have found that a car is too small for all their tailgating friends and supplies. They need something bigger. To solve this problem, many have done a little painting and welding and used a whole lot of imagination. I've seen fire trucks at Clemson, a fleet of black and gold buses at Appalachian State, and even a purple and gold bread truck in Baton Rouge. These custom vehicles are known throughout their campuses and are the perfect way for their owners to show team allegiance and to bring as many people and supplies as they want to their tailgate.

Cars with trailers, RVs, and buses serve fans well as ways to get to the tailgate, but many fans have found that, with college campuses covering hundreds of acres and traffic being a nightmare on game days, they need an alternative mode of transportation once they have arrived at their tailgating site. So, once the car, RV, or bus is parked, fans turn to custom-painted golf carts, bicycles, and even motorized coolers to visit friends' tailgates.

Cockaboose Railroad

In Columbia, South Carolina, tailgaters are allowed to use the South Carolina State Fairgrounds. The open parking lots and fields provide plenty of room for the thousands of South Carolina fans who come to support their team. However, it's what's behind Williams-Brice Stadium that makes tailgating in Columbia unique. Here sits a strip of old railroad tracks. On these tracks are twenty-two connected cabooses known as the Cockaboose Railroad. These aren't normal train cars. Rather, each has been transformed into a one-of-a-kind tailgating destination. Each Cockaboose car may look the same on the outside, but don't let that fool you. On the inside, each is unique. Complete with running water and electricity, these railcars have all the comforts of home, including bathrooms and kitchens. The interiors are decorated to each owner's taste. However, while the insides are beautifully decorated, most guests spend their time on top of the railcars watching earlier games on flat-screen TVs and grilling their game-day meals. Tailgating on top of a rail car provides an excellent vantage point for viewing the stadium and the thousands of tailgaters around it. Sound like something you would like to do? Get in line; acquiring a Cockaboose is a lengthy process. The Cockaboose Railroad operates like a condo association, and the only way to get one is to buy it from a current owner.

The Vol Navy

Almost all tailgaters spend their time before the game with their feet on solid ground. The exception is the fans who tailgate in Knoxville, Tennessee. Thanks to Neyland Stadium's close proximity to the Tennessee River, some tailgating in Tennessee takes place on water. On game day, dozens of boats will dock up behind the stadium. There, on the water, hundreds of "Vol Navy" members will conduct their pregame grilling, socializing, and celebrating. Like any tailgating group, members of the Vol Navy are passionate about their team. On game days, you'll see a variety of vessels: from smaller four-man boats all the way to yachts that dock up for the entire football season. During my first trip to Knoxville for game day, I was able to experience tailgating by water firsthand with Captain Keith Casey aboard his boat, the *Wastrel*.

On this trip, I discovered a certain serenity that comes with arriving by boat. I parked my car at the marina and enjoyed a peaceful hour-and-a-half ride to the stadium. Instead of spending time on congested highways and sitting in traffic, I was surrounded by the beautiful scenery of the nearby Smoky Mountains showing their fall colors. On arrival, all you do is dock up. After the game, you can continue your tailgate on board

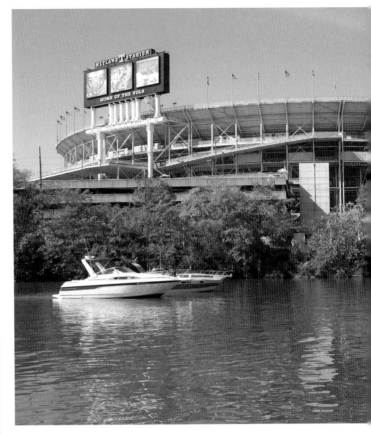

Members of the Vol Navy on their way to tailgate on the water outside Neyland Stadium in Knoxville, Tennessee

and avoid all postgame traffic by spending the night on the boat. The tailgating atmosphere with the Vol Navy is the same as it is on land: grills and kitchens are producing delicious food, TVs are showing the day's earlier games, and everyone is decked out in Tennessee orange. However, if you're throwing a football, be careful not to send it overboard.

Spending a game day on the water is a tailgating tradition that makes Tennessee unique. If you get a chance to tailgate with the Vol Navy, go for it! You won't regret it. ∎

Grilled Buttermilk Biscuits with Gingerbread Butter

Biscuit making in the South is something you learn from the previous generation. My mom learned from her grandmother, and I've learned from my mom. Making biscuits requires a feel for the dough. It's an art that comes only from experience. If you're a novice biscuit maker, you can use premade dough from the store for your biscuits, but remember that the only way to get better at making biscuits is to practice. I like my biscuits at a tailgate split in half, buttered, and grilled. Warm and crispy, they are wonderful spread with Gingerbread Butter.

MAKES 12 BISCUITS

Biscuits
6 cups self-rising flour
6 tablespoons vegetable shortening
6 tablespoons unsalted butter, very cold, cut into small pieces
2 1/2–2 3/4 cups buttermilk
1 stick unsalted butter, melted

Gingerbread Butter
2/3 cup dark brown sugar
1 tablespoon boiling water
2 sticks unsalted butter, softened
1/4 cup unsulphured molasses (like Grandma's Original)
1/4 cup finely chopped crystallized ginger
1/2 teaspoon powdered ginger
1/2 teaspoon ground cinnamon
1/4 teaspoon salt
1/4 teaspoon ground cloves
1/4 teaspoon grated orange zest

Preheat the oven to 400°.

In a large bowl, add the flour, shortening, and butter. Using a pastry blender, work quickly to cut the butter and shortening into the flour. Cut in an up-and-down motion while scraping down the sides of the bowl. Continue until the flour is a coarse, mealy texture.

Pour 2½ cups of buttermilk into the center of the bowl. With a fork, draw the flour in from all sides of the bowl, creating a shaggy dough. If the dough seems too dry, you may add up to ¼ cup more buttermilk. Bring the dough together, but be careful not to overwork it.

Place the biscuit dough on a floured surface. Dust your hands with flour and knead the dough 3 or 4 times, adding more flour if the dough begins to stick. Using a floured rolling pin, roll the dough in a single direction with light, even strokes to make a rectangle about 1½ inches thick.

Press a floured 3-inch biscuit cutter straight down into the dough. Be careful not to twist the cutter when you're pressing down, which will result in uneven biscuits. Place the biscuits on a lined baking sheet. Bake for 10–12 minutes, until golden brown. Let the biscuits cool and pack in a sealable container.

To make the Gingerbread Butter, put the brown sugar in a small bowl. Add the boiling water and stir to dissolve the sugar. It will be a thick paste.

In the bowl of a food processor, add the brown sugar mixture, butter, molasses, crystallized ginger, powdered ginger, cinnamon, salt, cloves, and orange zest. Pulse until the ingredients have formed a smooth, caramel-colored butter.

Remove the compound butter from the food processor bowl and place it in a sealable serving container. Cover and refrigerate over-night. Transport in a cooler to your tailgate. At the tailgate, remove the butter from the cooler and bring it to room temperature before serving.

To grill the biscuits at your tailgate, split each biscuit in half. Brush the cut side of each half with melted butter. Place on a medium grill with the buttered side down. Grill for 3–5 minutes, until crispy and golden brown. Serve with Gingerbread Butter.

Grilled Buttermilk Biscuits

Tailgating Families

Throughout my tailgating travels, I've experienced southern hospitality at its finest. I've been amazed at the openness of tailgaters across the South as they have invited me in, let me sample their food, and answered my questions about their game-day experiences. Tailgating is not a solo activity. It's definitely an activity in which "the more, the merrier" is the guiding principle. When tailgaters gather with each other in the same place every game day, they are what I like to call a "tailgating family." Whether or not they are actually related by blood makes no difference. On game days, tailgating families are all there for each other and for their team.

Forming a Family

When I meet new tailgating groups, I try to find out how the group formed. While the answers vary from campus to campus, many tailgaters have a similar story. Some began the tradition as undergrads. They gathered their friends, and their tailgate group grew throughout their time in school. Many fans are hooked on tailgating by the time they graduate. After graduation, tailgating brings college friends back together again. Every weekend in the fall is a chance for tailgaters to reunite with friends and family. If you're a student and enjoy game day, then start a tailgate with your friends. It doesn't have to be big. Get a small grill, bring some sides, and enjoy a pregame meal. It's a decision you won't regret. It could even be the start of a great tradition.

I've met some people who began tailgating when their children started college. Tailgating was a way for them to spend time with their grown children and to play host to them and their friends every game day. Often, those who start tailgating when their kids are in college continue long after they have graduated.

One of the largest groups of tailgaters is made up of life-long fans. Some have parents who were diehard fans; others are locals in the community where the campus is located. Whether or not they are alumni, life-long fans have a passion for their team that can be developed only through years of loyalty.

Regardless of how you start, it's in the social nature of tailgating to add new people every season. Some schools have assigned parking passes; other campuses have lots that are first-come, first-served. Tailgaters are creatures of habit, and once they find a spot they like, they'll return to the same spot every game. It's only natural that, after spending seven or so Saturdays together every fall, friendships with your tailgating neighbors would form. What starts out as a casual sharing of trash bags or a saltshaker can develop further over time. As the season passes, you'll likely grow close with the tailgaters you see every weekend. Your groups might join together and pool resources. A group that starts out as five or six people may grow into a group of dozens. There are advantages to consolidating resources. When tailgating funds are pooled, group members can split costs and acquire inflatable tents, generators, multiple flat-screen TVs, and even trailers with bathrooms.

Family Meetings

With some tailgating families serving over a hundred fans on game day, a high level of organization is necessary. Leaders are designated by some group founders to organize the season's tailgate. Over the summer, leaders plan out the upcoming season's menu, often using the game schedule as the inspiration for their game-day feasts, creatively collaborating to "eat the competition." Once the menu is planned, leaders will collect dues used to purchase the ingredients for the main dishes. On game day, individuals bring sides and desserts to share. Leaders and other designated members arrive early to set up the tents and begin cooking the main dishes before others arrive.

On my first trip to Appalachian State, I got to know the folks of Big C's Tailgate. When I returned later in the season for a playoff, I knew exactly where to find them, since tailgating families tend to have a specific spot where they spend every game. If a group outgrows a certain spot, members search for a larger area the next season. Larger groups mark their new territory by setting up several tents, flying a flag, or hanging a banner with the tailgating family name. Names can be anything from the last name of the host family to a creative description of where the group is located. For example, at LSU, I saw names ranging from "Ford Family Tailgating" to "Between the Mounds."

In-season organization is done through the use of websites, Facebook, and Twitter. Leaders are easily able to inform everyone in the group about the week's menu, what time they'll begin tailgating, and any other pertinent information. After the games, group leaders often post pictures and recipes from the day's tailgate.

These groups don't just get together for home games; they hit the road together. In Blacksburg, I met a tailgating group known as "The Valley Tribe of the Hokie Nation." Later in the season, I saw that members of the Valley Tribe had packed up their gear and made the trip to Charlotte together to cheer on their Hokies in the Atlantic Coast Conference Championship game.

Tailgating families that form among fans are something special. They may live in different towns or even states, but on game day, these tailgating families reunite to spend the day eating, drinking, and cheering on the team that brings them together in what's sometimes a decades-long tradition. ■

A member of the Valley Tribe shows off her group's koozies

Biscuits and Sawmill Gravy

Biscuits and Sawmill Gravy

Fluffy biscuits split in half with rich and creamy Sawmill Gravy ladled over the top is a meal that will feed even the heartiest of tailgating appetites. When tailgating, I like to make as many dishes as possible on-site. By measuring out my ingredients the night before, I have everything I need to make fresh gravy at my tailgate.

MAKES 12 SERVINGS

4 tablespoons all-purpose flour
½ teaspoon McCormick Coarse Ground Black Pepper
½ teaspoon salt
2 cups whole milk
1 cup half-and-half
⅛ teaspoon Tabasco sauce
1 pound bulk sausage

The night before your tailgate, measure out the flour, pepper, and salt and store in a sealable plastic bag. Place the milk, half-and-half, and Tabasco in a sealable container and refrigerate overnight. Transport the milk mixture and sausage in a cooler to the tailgate.

Heat a medium-sized pan over a burner. Add the sausage and cook over medium heat. While cooking, break up the sausage into bite-sized pieces. Once the sausage has cooked to a crispy golden brown, add the flour mixture to the skillet and cook for 3 minutes over medium-low heat, stirring frequently.

Pour in the milk mixture ½ cup at a time, stirring after each addition until incorporated. Raise the heat to medium and cook the gravy for 7–10 minutes, until desired thickness is reached. Serve over Grilled Buttermilk Biscuits (page 48) or Potato Hash (page 54). The gravy can be held for a while over very low heat. Stir before serving.

Potato Hash

On Saturday mornings in college, after a 10,000-yard swim practice, a scrambler from Mickies Dairy Bar in Madison, Wisconsin, provided me with the fuel necessary for a day of tailgating and an evening game. The scrambler is a towering heap of eggs, bacon, cheese, and gravy sitting on top of Potato Hash. If you're looking for a solid foundation for your tailgating breakfast spread, then look no further than Potato Hash. The potatoes can be made the day before and then crisped up on-site.

MAKES 8 SERVINGS

8 cups peeled and chopped Yukon Gold potatoes
3½ teaspoons salt, divided
8 tablespoons unsalted butter, divided
1 cup chopped yellow onions
½ cup chopped shallots
2 tablespoons seeded and chopped jalapeño peppers
3 cups chopped mixed peppers (any combination of red, yellow, green, orange, poblano, and cubanelle)
1 teaspoon minced garlic
1 teaspoon McCormick Coarse Ground Black Pepper

In a large pot, add the potatoes and cover with cold water. Bring the water to a boil. Add 1½ teaspoons salt and reduce heat to a simmer. Cook until the potatoes are fork tender. Drain the water and return the potatoes to the pot. Cover the top of the pot with a clean dishcloth and let cool.

In a large skillet, add 4 tablespoons of the unsalted butter. Add the onions, shallots, peppers, and garlic. Cook over medium heat until the onions and peppers soften.

In a large aluminum roasting pan, add the potatoes, onions, peppers, and garlic. Toss together and season with 2 teaspoons of the salt and the pepper. Cover the pan with plastic wrap and refrigerate overnight. Transport to your tailgate in a cooler.

When ready to serve at your tailgate, heat the remaining 4 tablespoons of butter in a pan over a burner. When the pan is hot, add the

Potato Hash

potatoes and cook over medium heat to warm them up. Increase heat to medium-high until the potatoes have reached the desired level of browning.

Once browned, remove from the pan and serve. Top with cheese, salsa, eggs, or any other breakfast item you choose.

Tex-Mex Scrambled Eggs on Grilled Potato Skins

Filled with bacon and eggs and the Tex-Mex flavors of peppers, cumin, and chipotle, this dish will warm you from the inside out. These eggs are great on their own, in a tortilla, or on a biscuit. My favorite way to eat them is on a grilled potato skin. This is the ultimate grab-and-go breakfast item.

MAKES 10–12 SERVINGS

Eggs

1 pound thick-cut bacon

4 tablespoons unsalted butter

½ cup chopped cubanelle peppers

½ cup chopped orange bell peppers

½ cup chopped yellow onions

1 cup red grape tomatoes, quartered lengthwise

8 ounces grated chipotle Gouda cheese

12 large eggs

½ teaspoon salt

½ teaspoon ground cumin

¼ teaspoon McCormick Coarse Ground Black Pepper

Grilled Potato Skins (makes 24 potato skins)

12 russet baking potatoes

1 stick unsalted butter

½ teaspoon salt

½ teaspoon ground cumin

½ teaspoon McCormick Coarse Ground Black Pepper

The night before the tailgate, cook the bacon and then drain on paper towels. Chop into bite-sized pieces and store in a sealable container. Place the 4 tablespoons of butter in a sealable container. Place the peppers and onions in a sealable container. Place the grape tomatoes in a sealable container. Store the cheese in a sealable container. Refrigerate all the containers overnight.

In a medium-sized bowl, add the eggs use a fork to break up the yolks and whites. Add the salt, cumin, and pepper and stir. Transfer the egg mixture to a sealable container and refrigerate overnight.

Preheat the oven to 400°. Wash and dry the potatoes and pierce each with a fork. Place the potatoes on a baking sheet. Bake until cooked through, about 50 minutes. Let the potatoes cool for 15 minutes. Slice each in half lengthwise. Remove the insides of the potato with a spoon, leaving about ¼ inch of potato on each skin. Store the potato skins in a sealable container and refrigerate overnight. Place the stick of unsalted butter, salt, cumin, and pepper in a sealable container and refrigerate overnight.

The morning of the tailgate, transport the refrigerated containers in a cooler to your tailgate.

At your tailgate, melt the butter, salt, cumin, and pepper in a pot over medium heat. Brush the melted butter mixture on all sides of the potato skins. Place the buttered skins on a metal baking sheet, cut-side down, and place the baking sheet on a medium grill. Close the grill and cook for about 5 minutes, until the butter bubbles and the skins begin to brown. Flip the skins over and cook for about 5 more minutes, until the skins are browned all over. Remove the pan from the heat.

Prepare the eggs by adding the 4 tablespoons of butter to a medium-sized sauté pan. Melt over medium heat. Increase to medium-high and cook bacon pieces, peppers, onions, and tomatoes for 5 minutes, stirring frequently. Mix together the egg and seasoning mixture and add to the pan. Cook the eggs, stirring over medium-high heat until just scrambled. Remove the eggs from heat.

Add a layer of chipotle Gouda to the Grilled Potato Skins, then fill them with Tex-Mex Scrambled Eggs.

Tex-Mex Scrambled Eggs on Grilled Potato Skins

Pepper and Hot Sausage Grits

Loaded with hot sausage, sautéed bell peppers, and Pepper Jack cheese, this recipe transforms grits from a side dish to a tailgating brunch staple. It'll help warm you up on any cool game-day morning.

MAKES 10 SERVINGS

1 cup diced yellow onions
1 cup diced bell peppers
4 cups water
4 cups whole milk
1 cup heavy cream
1½ teaspoons salt, divided
8 ounces grated Pepper Jack cheese
2 cups white or yellow cleaned grits
¼ teaspoon McCormick Coarse Ground Black Pepper
1 pound hot bulk ground sausage

The night before the tailgate, pack the onions and peppers in separate sealable containers. Pack the water, milk, cream, and 1 teaspoon of the salt in a sealable container. Pack the cheese in a separate sealable container. Refrigerate these containers overnight and transport in a cooler to your tailgate. Pack the grits in a sealable container and ½ teaspoon of the salt and the pepper in a separate container.

If you have two propane burners at your tailgate, you can cook the sausage and grits at the same time. If not, then cook the sausage first, followed by the grits.

In a medium-sized frying pan, cook the sausage over medium heat, breaking it into small pieces while cooking. Once the sausage is browned, add the onions and peppers and cook until the onions are translucent and the peppers are soft. Remove from heat.

In a heavy-bottomed pot, add the water, milk, cream, and salt. Bring the pot to a simmer and turn the heat to very low. Add the grits, stir, and cover. Cook for 15–20 minutes, stirring often, until the grits are a creamy consistency.

Once the grits are cooked, add the sausage, onion, and pepper mix; cheese; and ½ teaspoon of the salt and the pepper. Stir, mixing all ingredients together. Remove from heat and serve.

An assortment of pregame snacks and appetizers at your tailgate allows guests to always have something available to munch on when they stop by. Many appetizers are dual-purpose and can be used later as condiments for your main dish. When serving hummus, salsas, or cheese balls, I like to offer my guests several choices. If you tailgate with a smaller crowd, then you can try different flavor combinations at different games throughout the season. If you're a guest at a tailgate, bringing one of these appetizers or snacks to share is something your host will appreciate.

Appetizers & Snacks

Carrot Hummus, Chameleon Hummus (p. 62), and Jalapeño Hummus (p. 63)

Carrot Hummus

A carrot-flavored hummus might sound strange, but once your guests try it, you'll understand why it's one of my family's favorites. Fans of Clemson, Virginia, Auburn, or any other orange-colored school will find that this pale-orange hummus coordinates beautifully with your tailgating spread.

MAKES ABOUT 5 CUPS

1 cup chopped carrots
2 (15 1/2-ounce) cans of garbanzo beans, drained,
    liquid reserved
1/2 cup tahini
6 tablespoons lemon juice
3 tablespoons olive oil
1 tablespoon chopped garlic
1 1/4 teaspoons salt
1 teaspoon paprika
1 teaspoon grated lemon zest
1/2 teaspoon grated orange zest
1/2 teaspoon Tabasco sauce
1/4 teaspoon ground cumin
1/8 teaspoon ground cloves
1 cup grated carrots

In a small saucepan over medium-high heat, cook the chopped carrots in water to cover until fork tender. Drain and add to the bowl of a food processor.

Add the garbanzo beans, 4 tablespoons of the reserved bean liquid, tahini, lemon juice, olive oil, garlic, salt, paprika, lemon and orange zest, Tabasco, cumin, and cloves. Process until an orange hummus of desired smoothness forms. If it's too thick, you may add additional bean liquid or olive oil until the desired consistency is reached.

Add the grated carrots and pulse a few times until evenly mixed into the hummus. Store in the refrigerator overnight. On game day, keep in a cooler until ready to use. Serve with apple slices that have been tossed in lemon juice and sprinkled with McCormick Coarse Ground Black Pepper.

Chameleon Hummus

Traditional hummus can be made to show support for any team. Like a chameleon that blends in with its surroundings, this hummus can fit in at any divided tailgate with the addition of green, red, yellow, orange, or purple bell peppers. Avoid an argument by having hummus to suit both loyalties. In the state of Alabama, Auburn fans can add orange bell peppers and Alabama fans can add red. That way everybody wins.

MAKES ABOUT 5 CUPS

2 ($15\frac{1}{2}$-ounce) cans of garbanzo beans, drained,
   liquid reserved
$\frac{1}{2}$ cup tahini
6 tablespoons lemon juice
3 tablespoons olive oil
1 tablespoon chopped garlic
$1\frac{1}{2}$ teaspoons grated lemon zest
$1\frac{1}{4}$ teaspoon salt
$\frac{1}{2}$ teaspoon Tabasco sauce
$\frac{1}{4}$ teaspoon cumin
$1\frac{1}{2}$ cups diced bell peppers, your choice of color

In the bowl of a food processor, add the garbanzo beans, 6 tablespoons of the reserved bean liquid, tahini, lemon juice, olive oil, garlic, lemon zest, salt, Tabasco, and cumin. Process until the hummus reaches the desired smoothness.

Empty the hummus into a sealable container. Fold in the peppers. Store in the refrigerator overnight. On game day, keep in a cooler until ready to use.

Jalapeño Hummus

If you enjoy food with a little kick, Jalapeño Hummus is for you. The pale-green color may make this hummus look mild, but the jalapeño heat will be sure to leave anyone with bold taste buds happy. For those with a milder palate, you can always adjust the amount of jalapeño used.

MAKES ABOUT 5 CUPS

3 tablespoons olive oil
1/2 cup seeded and roughly chopped jalapeño peppers
1/2 cup seeded and roughly chopped poblano peppers
3 1/2 teaspoons chopped garlic
2 (15 1/2-ounce) cans of garbanzo beans, drained,
    liquid reserved
1/2 cup tahini
6 tablespoons lemon juice
1 tablespoon lime juice
1 1/4 teaspoon salt
1 teaspoon grated lemon zest
1/2 teaspoon grated lime zest
1/2 teaspoon Tabasco sauce
1/2 teaspoon cumin
1/2 cup chopped cilantro leaves

In a nonstick pan, add the olive oil, peppers, and garlic. Cook over medium heat until the peppers soften, about 3–5 minutes.

In the bowl of a food processor, add the garbanzo beans, 4 tablespoons of the reserved bean liquid, tahini, lemon juice, lime juice, salt, lemon and lime zest, Tabasco, cumin, and sautéed peppers. Process until the hummus reaches the desired smoothness.

Add the cilantro and pulse a few times until it's incorporated. Store in the refrigerator overnight. On game day, keep in a cooler until ready to use.

Granny Smith Apple Salsa

When you think of salsa, is pico de gallo the first kind that comes to mind? This combination of tomatoes, onions, and peppers works as an appetizer with chips or as a condiment for tacos and burgers. If you're looking for a salsa that's a little different from what you're used to, try this one. It's more tart than what you'll find at most tailgates because of the Granny Smith apples in it.

MAKES ABOUT 7 CUPS

½ cup fresh lime juice
1½ cups diced Granny Smith apples
5 cups seeded and chopped Roma tomatoes,
    drained on paper towels
1 cup chopped cilantro leaves
1 cup chopped yellow onions
¾ cup seeded and diced poblano peppers
¼ cup seeded and finely diced jalapeño peppers
½ cup chopped shallots
1 tablespoon grated lime zest
1 teaspoon salt
¼ teaspoon McCormick Coarse Ground Black Pepper

As soon as you've diced the apples, place them with the lime juice in a medium-sized bowl and stir.

In a large bowl, add the rest of the ingredients. Stir in the apples and lime juice until all ingredients are evenly mixed together. Store in a sealable container and refrigerate overnight. On game day, keep in a cooler until ready to serve. Stir again before serving.

Granny Smith Apple Salsa,
Pineapple and Yellow Tomato
Salsa (p. 66), and Black Bean
and Corn Salsa (p. 67)

Pineapple and Yellow Tomato Salsa

This salsa takes advantage of the yellow tomatoes still found at farmers' markets during the beginning of football season. The addition of pineapple and jalapeños makes a salsa that's sweet with a little bit of heat. This combination creates a refreshing flavor that's great with chips or as a topper for grilled meats or sandwiches.

MAKES ABOUT 7 CUPS

3 cups chopped fresh pineapple
1 cup chopped and seeded yellow tomatoes,
    drained on paper towels
1 cup chopped red bell peppers
1 cup chopped orange bell peppers
½ cup chopped cilantro leaves
¼ cup chopped shallots
3 tablespoons seeded and chopped jalapeño peppers
2 teaspoons minced garlic
¼ cup fresh lime juice
1 teaspoon grated lime zest
½ teaspoon salt
¼ teaspoon McCormick Coarse Ground Black Pepper

Add all the ingredients to a medium-sized bowl. Stir until evenly mixed. Store in a sealable container and refrigerate overnight. On game day, keep in a cooler until ready to serve. Stir prior to serving.

Black Bean and Corn Salsa

This has always been my go-to salsa. It's on the table every time I host a tailgate. It's easy to prepare and tastes great any time of year. But be careful—if you stand within reach of it for too long, you could end up too full to eat anything else!

MAKES ABOUT 7 CUPS

2 (15-ounce) cans of black beans

1 (19-ounce) can of garbanzo beans

1 (11-ounce) can of sweet corn kernels

2 (10-ounce) cans of Rotel tomatoes with lime and cilantro

1 cup diced red bell peppers

1 cup diced green bell peppers

¼ cup minced onions

2 tablespoons lime juice

2 teaspoons grated lime zest

1 teaspoon minced garlic

1 teaspoon salt

¼ teaspoon McCormick Coarse Ground Black Pepper

1½ cups chopped cilantro leaves

Drain all canned ingredients and add to a large bowl. Add the peppers, onions, lime juice, lime zest, garlic, salt, and pepper. Stir until evenly mixed together. Toss in the cilantro. Store in a sealable container and refrigerate overnight. On game day, keep in a cooler until ready to serve. Stir before serving.

Brandy-Almond-Brie Cheese Ball, Bacon–Blue Cheese Ball (p. 70), and Pimento Cheese Ball (p. 71)

Brandy-Almond-Brie Cheese Ball

Are you looking for a sophisticated appetizer to match your tailgate's chandelier and silver chafing dishes? This Brandy-Almond-Brie Cheese Ball will look incredibly appetizing on a silver platter. The creamy, buttery flavor of the Brie and the nuttiness of the almond coating are a wonderful pairing that will keep your guests coming back for more.

MAKES 6–8 SERVINGS

1 pound Brie, outer rind removed
1 stick unsalted butter, softened
4 ounces cream cheese, softened
2 tablespoons Cognac
½ teaspoon dried thyme
½ teaspoon salt
⅛ teaspoon Tabasco sauce
1 cup slivered almonds, lightly toasted
1½ cups sliced almonds, lightly toasted

Place the Brie, butter, cream cheese, Cognac, thyme, salt, and Tabasco in the bowl of a food processor. Pulse until the ingredients are combined into a smooth and creamy mixture. Add the slivered almonds and pulse a few times to incorporate into the rest of the mixture.

Line the bottom of a small bowl with plastic wrap. Remove the mixture from the food processor and place in the lined bowl. Cover and chill in the refrigerator until firm, about 3 hours.

Once firm, use the plastic wrap to shape the cheese into a ball and then remove the mixture from the plastic wrap. Roll the cheese ball in the sliced almonds, pressing down so the almonds adhere to the entire surface. Wrap in plastic wrap and refrigerate. The cheese ball can be made up to 3 days before the game. Transport to the game in a cooler and serve upon arrival.

Bacon–Blue Cheese Ball

Did you know that Clemson University makes its own blue cheese? If you aren't an alumnus, you might not have known that handmade blue cheese is sold in the dining hall and is available to be shipped around the country. For a Clemson fan, no tailgate is complete without the school's blue cheese on the table. The Bacon–Blue Cheese Ball is great on crackers or crumbled on top of a burger.

MAKES 6–8 SERVINGS

5 slices of thick-cut bacon
8 ounces cream cheese, softened
4 ounces blue cheese, crumbled
4 ounces grated sharp white cheddar cheese
1 tablespoon lemon juice
$\frac{1}{4}$ teaspoon Tabasco sauce
$\frac{1}{8}$ teaspoon McCormick Coarse Ground Black Pepper
$\frac{1}{8}$ teaspoon garlic powder
$1\frac{1}{2}$ cups chopped, toasted walnuts

Cook the bacon until crisp. Remove from the pan and let drain on paper towels, then crumble into small pieces. Place the bacon crumbles, cream cheese, blue cheese, cheddar cheese, lemon juice, Tabasco, pepper, and garlic powder in the bowl of a food processor. Pulse until the ingredients are combined into a smooth and creamy mixture.

Line the bottom of a small bowl with plastic wrap. Remove the mixture from the food processor and place in the lined bowl. Cover and chill in the refrigerator until firm, about 3 hours.

Once firm, use the plastic wrap to shape the cheese into a ball and then remove the mixture from the plastic wrap. Roll the cheese ball in the chopped walnuts, pressing down with enough pressure so the walnuts adhere to the entire surface. Wrap the cheese ball in plastic wrap and refrigerate overnight. The cheese ball can be made up to 3 days before the tailgate. Transport it to the game in a cooler and serve upon arrival.

Pimento Cheese Ball

Serving pimento cheese in a pecan-crusted cheese ball is a new way to present this classic spread at your tailgate. Slicing off a piece and spreading it on a cracker allows guests to have both crunchy-nutty and creamy-cheesy textures in one bite.

MAKES 6–8 SERVINGS

3 ounces pimentos
3 ½ cups grated extra sharp cheddar cheese
6 ounces cream cheese, softened
4 ½ teaspoons lemon juice
1 tablespoon grated yellow onions
2 ¼ teaspoons Worcestershire sauce
⅜ teaspoon salt
⅜ teaspoon dry mustard
¼ teaspoon Tabasco sauce
1 ½ cups chopped, toasted pecans

Drain the pimentos and chop. Pat dry with paper towels, removing as much liquid as possible. In the bowl of a food processor, add the cheddar cheese, cream cheese, lemon juice, onions, Worcestershire, salt, mustard, and Tabasco. Pulse until a smooth and creamy mixture is formed. Add the pimentos and pulse until blended.

Line the bottom of a small bowl with plastic wrap. Remove the mixture from the food processor and place in the lined bowl. Cover and chill in the refrigerator until the mixture is firm, about 3 hours.

Once firm, use the plastic wrap to shape the cheese into a ball and then remove the mixture from the plastic wrap. Roll the cheese ball in the pecans, pressing down lightly so the pecans adhere to the entire surface. Wrap the ball in plastic wrap and refrigerate overnight. This cheese ball can be made up to 3 days before the tailgate. Transport to the game in a cooler and serve upon arrival.

College-Town Restaurants and Tailgating

Every weekend in the fall, thousands of college football fans migrate to their team's home stadium. Smaller communities—like Oxford, Mississippi; Clemson, South Carolina; and Auburn, Alabama—swell in size. Every hotel within an hour's drive will be booked up. When tailgaters travel for a game, they aren't on campus just for the day; they make a weekend out of it.

All tailgaters are glad to be on campus, and regardless of how often they return, many fans spend game day eve visiting the bars and restaurants that are special to them. Restaurants come and go, but every campus has a place that you know will be there forever. This campus landmark is much more than a place to eat. It's the place where you went on first dates or where, as a kid, your dad took you before catching a game and to which you want to introduce your own children. Throughout my game-day travels, I've had the pleasure of spending many Fridays at restaurants such as these. Here are a few of my favorite places to visit on game-day weekend.

Mario's Fishbowl in Morgantown, West Virginia

If you're at all confused by the name, take one step into Mario's and you'll quickly realize this isn't a pet store. The only fish you'll find here is fried. The walls are lined with hundreds of notes from former patrons expressing their pride in West Virginia University. First opened in 1963, this campus icon is famous for its "fishbowls" of beer. These goblets of beer come in a variety of sizes and can quench the largest of thirsts. For a celebration like game day, a normal glass won't do. Drinking a fishbowl of your favorite beer surrounded by fellow fans creates an atmosphere that would make anyone excited for the next day. Make sure you get to Mario's early on Friday before a game. The place will quickly become standing room only, filled with fans eager to cheer WVU on to victory.

The Varsity in Atlanta, Georgia

Georgia Tech's campus sits in the heart of the hustle and bustle of Atlanta. This urban tailgating experience is very different from what you'll find elsewhere. On one side of I-85 sits Bobby Dodd Stadium. On the other side sits the world's largest drive-in, The Varsity. Since 1928, Georgia Tech fans have been enjoying The Varsity's chili cheese dogs, onion rings, and frosted orange. On game day, thousands of fans will make their way through The Varsity's doors. If you take a seat in the back, you can look out across the interstate and see into Bobby Dodd Stadium.

Rama Jama's in Tuscaloosa, Alabama

It's hard not to notice this Tuscaloosa icon located across the street from Bryant-Denny Stadium. The archetype of a game-day restaurant, Rama Jama's is lined from floor to ceiling with Crimson Tide football images, programs, and autographed memorabilia. If it weren't for the delicious smells coming from the grill, it would be easy to spend hours examining every artifact of Alabama football history. To order, you walk up to the counter and choose from the items on three large blackboards. The menu has everything from breakfast to National Championship–inspired burgers with a slice of bacon for every national championship won. With the food and interior overflowing with enthusiasm about Alabama football, it's impossible to dine

Rama Jama's in Tuscaloosa, Alabama

here on a Friday and not get excited about the next day's game.

Pancake Pantry in Nashville, Tennessee

Nashville, home to Vanderbilt University, is larger than many traditional college towns and has a variety of restaurants favored by college students. Located across the street from Vanderbilt's campus, the Pancake Pantry is the perfect place for a Sunday morning breakfast before leaving town after a game. Since 1961, the Pancake Pantry has been cooking a wide assortment of delicious pancakes, using a proprietary blend of eastern Tennessee–ground flour and house-made syrups. With over twenty different types of pancakes on the menu, ordering may seem daunting. Just remember, you can't go wrong with old-fashioned buttermilk pancakes.

Taylor Grocery in Taylor, Mississippi

Several miles outside of Oxford is the tiny town of Taylor. It's home to some of the best catfish I've ever eaten. At Taylor Grocery, the motto is "Eat or We Both Starve." Ole Miss fans take this to heart and will wait hours to dine on a cat-

fish platter, fried okra, chocolate cobbler, and other southern delicacies. On Friday evenings before a game, the parking lot and porch of the 100-plus-year-old building are filled. Stories of past game-day weekends are exchanged, and predictions of what will happen on the field this season will be made. Game-day weekend attracts a crowd, but in that atmosphere it doesn't seem like a wait at all. Inside the restaurant, the walls are covered with signatures of past patrons, including Ole Miss great Eli Manning.

The Esso Club in Clemson, South Carolina

Across the street from Clemson's Memorial Stadium is the Esso Club. Decades ago, the Esso Club started out as a gas station and has, over the years, turned into one of the most popular bars on campus. On game day, its parking lot turns into one giant party. Throughout the day, hundreds of Clemson fans fill the parking lot to have a drink and meet up before the game. If you aren't tailgating on game day, there's a good chance you'll be at the Esso. When you're there, make sure to try the fried pickle spears. ■

Grill-Spiced Pecans

My tailgating version of spiced pecans adds an element of fun to this party snack staple. Why make them at home when you can easily make them on your grill? While the grill is heating up for your main dish, you can provide guests with freshly roasted spiced pecans and an experience they won't soon forget.

MAKES ABOUT 3 CUPS

3 cups pecan halves
4 tablespoons unsalted butter
½ cup sugar
½ teaspoon salt
¼ teaspoon ground cloves
¼ teaspoon cayenne pepper
¼ teaspoon black pepper

At home, measure out the pecans and store in a sealable container. Pack the butter in a small sealable container and refrigerate overnight. Add the rest of the ingredients to a small sealable container and mix together.

At your tailgate, place a 9 × 13-inch baking pan over a medium-high grill. Add the butter and let it melt. Once the butter is melted, add the pecans and stir, making sure all the nuts are covered in melted butter.

Add about half of the spice mix to the pan and stir. Cook the pecans over a medium-high grill, stirring frequently for about 8 minutes. Remove from heat and add the remaining spice mix. Stir to evenly coat. Transfer to a serving bowl or place the pan on a trivet and serve.

Grill-Spiced Pecans

Harry's Hot Balls

You know a dish is a family favorite when, despite the fact that it almost caused the house to burn down, it's still made. When I was growing up, there was an incident with this recipe in which the oven was set to "broil" rather than to "bake." A visit from the fire department and one oven later, sausage balls remain one of my family's favorite breakfast foods. During my brother Harrison's time at the University of South Carolina, he developed a tailgating version that has now become a game-day tradition.

MAKES 24–30 BALLS

2 cups Bisquick
2 cups grated extra sharp cheddar cheese
½ cup seeded and finely chopped jalapeño peppers
½ cup chopped scallions (white and green parts)
⅓ cup finely chopped green bell peppers
1 pound bulk hot sausage
⅓ cup chipotle Tabasco sauce

Preheat the oven to at 350°.

In a large bowl, mix together the Bisquick, cheese, jalapeños, scallions, and peppers. Tear the sausage into small pieces and place in the bowl. Add the Tabasco. Mix by hand until the ingredients are evenly distributed.

Pinch off a small piece of dough and place it in the palm of your hand. Roll it between your hands to form a 1-inch-sized ball. Continue until all the dough is used. Place the sausage balls on a lined baking sheet and bake for 18–20 minutes until golden brown. Let the sausage balls cool. Remove from the baking sheet and store in a sealable container. Upon arriving at your tailgate, set the sausage balls out so your guests can enjoy them throughout the day.

Sweet-and-Savory Snack Mix

If you're enjoying some beverages at your tailgate, you may not be hungry, but you'll begin to crave something to excite your taste buds. If you need a crunchy finger-food snack you can quickly enjoy, this Sweet-and-Savory Snack Mix is just what you've been looking for.

MAKES 8–12 SERVINGS

3 cups crispy wheat cereal squares
3 cups crispy corn cereal squares
3 cups toasted oat O-shaped cereal
3 cups oyster crackers
1 stick unsalted butter, melted
2 teaspoons salt
$\frac{1}{2}$ teaspoon black pepper
$\frac{1}{2}$ teaspoon dried thyme
$\frac{1}{4}$ teaspoon ground coriander
3 cups golden raisins
$1\frac{1}{4}$ cups butterscotch morsels

Preheat the oven to 250°.

In a large bowl, stir together the cereal and crackers. In a small bowl, stir together the melted butter, salt, pepper, thyme, and coriander. Add the butter mixture to the cereal and crackers. Toss together, coating all the dry ingredients with the butter mixture.

Spread the mix in a single layer on 2 baking sheets. Bake for 1 hour, stirring the mix and turning the pans every 15 minutes. Remove from the oven and cool. Place in a large serving bowl and toss with the raisins and butterscotch morsels. Transport to the tailgate in the covered bowl. Allow guests to serve themselves by scooping the mix into small cups.

Cheddar and Pecan Cookies

Don't let the name "cookie" fool you. These sharp cheddar and pecan snacks bring the heat, not the sweet, to your tailgate. The beauty of this dough is that you don't have to chill it before rolling it out—perfect for the time-strapped tailgating chef.

MAKES ABOUT 8 DOZEN 2-INCH COOKIES

2 sticks unsalted butter, softened
1 pound grated extra sharp cheddar cheese
3 $\frac{1}{2}$ cups sifted cake flour, divided
1 $\frac{1}{4}$ teaspoons cayenne pepper
1 teaspoon salt
1 teaspoon paprika
1 $\frac{1}{2}$ cups pecan halves
3 tablespoons unsalted butter, melted

Preheat the oven to 375°.

Add the softened butter and cheese to the bowl of a food processor and pulse until blended. Add 3 cups of the sifted cake flour, cayenne pepper, salt, and paprika to a medium-sized bowl. Stir to mix together. Add half of the flour mixture to the cheese and butter mixture and pulse until the flour is blended. Add the remaining half of the flour mixture and pulse until blended. Remove the dough from the mixer. It should be the consistency of children's modeling clay.

Divide the dough in half. Sprinkle the rolling surface with some of the remaining sifted cake flour. Roll half of the dough to $\frac{1}{4}$-inch thickness. Using a 2-inch circular cookie cutter, cut the dough into circles. Place the cut-out cookies on lined baking sheets. Toss the pecan halves with the melted butter. Lightly press one pecan half in the center of each cookie. Bake for 12–14 minutes, until the cookies are just beginning to brown around the edges. Repeat the process with the remaining dough. Cool the cookies on wire racks before storing in a sealable container and bringing to your tailgate.

Cheddar and Pecan Cookies

Quick Pickle Platter

A platter of quick pickles is a beautiful side dish to have on game day. An assortment of pickled produce in different-sized jars is an inviting and intriguing snack to have on your tailgating table. Quick pickles serve a variety of functions: they can be used as a snack, as a topping for sandwiches, or in your Bloody Mary Bar (page 22). I've included two different pickling solutions. The White Vinegar Pickle is delicious with cucumbers, zucchini, and green beans. The Apple Cider Vinegar Pickle pairs with carrots, beets, and onions.

MAKES 10–12 SERVINGS

White Vinegar Pickle
Green beans and zucchini or cucumbers, cut into spears
2 cups white vinegar
$\frac{1}{2}$ cup water
5 tablespoons sugar
2 teaspoons salt
$\frac{1}{4}$ teaspoon McCormick Coarse Ground Black Pepper

Apple Cider Vinegar Pickle
Whole baby carrots and peeled beets and onions cut into bite-sized pieces
2 cups apple cider vinegar
$\frac{1}{2}$ cup apple juice
2 tablespoons chopped crystallized ginger
2 tablespoons dark brown sugar
2 tablespoons light brown sugar
$1\frac{1}{2}$ teaspoons salt
1 teaspoon whole peppercorns
1 teaspoon coriander seeds

Zucchini, baby carrot, pearl onion, radish, and beet pickles

Place vegetables of the same size in clean sealable glass jars.

For the White Vinegar Pickle, add the white vinegar, water, sugar, salt, and pepper to a medium-size pot.

For the Apple Cider Vinegar Pickle, add the apple cider vinegar, apple juice, crystallized ginger, dark brown sugar, light brown sugar, salt, peppercorns, and coriander seeds to a medium-size pot.

Bring the liquid to a simmer and stir until the sugar is dissolved. Remove from heat. Pour the hot liquid into the jars to cover the vegetables. Let the jars cool. Seal and refrigerate for 24 hours prior to serving. Serve with toothpicks or forks so your guests can help themselves.

Lemon-Parmesan Dip

This versatile appetizer will serve a variety of roles at your game-day spread. It can be served as a dip for vegetables and chips. Later, guests will find the bright and refreshing balance of lemon and parmesan a delicious accompaniment to chicken or pork sandwiches.

MAKES ABOUT 3 CUPS

2 cups sour cream

4 ounces cream cheese, softened

2 tablespoons lemon juice

1 tablespoon grated lemon zest

1 $\frac{1}{3}$ cups grated Parmesan cheese

1 teaspoon dried tarragon

$\frac{1}{2}$ teaspoon salt

$\frac{1}{4}$ teaspoon Tabasco sauce

Place all the ingredients in the bowl of a food processor. Process until smooth and creamy. Transfer to a sealable container and refrigerate overnight. Transport in a cooler to your tailgate. Upon arriving, serve on a platter with chips or an assortment of cut vegetables.

Sherwood's Anything Dip

Looks can be deceiving. This beautiful pale green dip has surprisingly bold flavors. Named Anything Dip because it goes with anything and everything, it's a great dipping sauce with Harry's Hot Balls (page 76), chips, or a wide assortment of vegetables and chips.

MAKES 2 CUPS

3 tablespoons unsalted butter

¼ cup chopped scallions (white and green parts)

2 tablespoons finely chopped yellow onions

3 tablespoons finely chopped and seeded jalapeño peppers

3 tablespoons finely chopped poblano peppers

3 tablespoons finely chopped cubanelle peppers

3 tablespoons finely chopped garlic

1 cup mayonnaise

1 cup sour cream

1 teaspoon green Tabasco sauce

1 teaspoon Tabasco sauce

¾ teaspoon salt

½ teaspoon McCormick Coarse Ground Black Pepper

½ teaspoon grated lime zest

In a medium sauté pan, melt the butter. Add the scallions, onions, peppers, and garlic and cook on medium-low heat for 5 minutes. Remove from heat. Cool.

Add the mayonnaise and sour cream to the bowl of a food processor. Add the green Tabasco, Tabasco, salt, pepper, and lime zest and process to blend. Add the onion and pepper mixture. Pulse just until the ingredients are bended. Remove from the bowl and store in a sealable container. Refrigerate overnight and transport in a cooler to your tailgate.

The All-Day Tailgate

Many southern college towns are smaller communities that grow and flourish along with the university in their midst. Over time, as the school grows in size, the community also expands. This growth and change happen gradually, but what happens on Saturdays in the fall is anything but gradual.

The enormity of a college football game day is impossible for a community not to notice. On the campuses of Clemson, Ole Miss, Mississippi State, and Auburn, the stadiums seat more than the population of the town. In Knoxville, Tuscaloosa, and Austin, over 100,000 fans fill the stands on Saturdays. At West Virginia University, when Milan Puskar Stadium is filled, it's the largest "city" in the entire state. The impact of game day isn't felt only at large Division I schools but also at the smallest of schools. Hampden-Sydney, Virginia, is a town of fewer than 2,000 residents, but the average attendance of HSC's football games is over 7,000. No matter the size of the school, dozens of college towns double or even triple their populations on game day.

This increase in size leads to one major problem: traffic. Roads meant for a town of a few thousand experience nothing but gridlock before and after kickoff. A tailgater's solution to this problem is the all-day tailgate. A fan at Clemson put it best, describing tailgating all day as more of a marathon than a sprint. Auburn fan Amanda Pair has a great strategy: "We usually tailgate all day before a game, so we like lots of heavy appetizers that keep you full till game time." Some tailgaters serve lighter appetizers in the morning and the larger main entrée before kickoff. After the game, you can finish up with a sandwich or two before driving home.

Since many tailgaters have a satellite dish and TV at their tailgate, they'll spend the day watching the noon, midafternoon, and evening games all from their tailgating spot. Most college lots stay open for twelve hours or more on game day, so you may find yourself spending over half of your Saturday on campus. ∎

Tailgaters in West Virginia's Blue Lot at the end of a full day of tailgating

Hot Ham Rolls

Ham rolls are a classic appetizer generally made of ham, swiss cheese, and mustard sauce. At Emory & Henry College, I saw them baked ahead of time and served cold. My take on this delicious party food requires a grill. Wrapping these rolls in foil and grilling them for a few minutes on each side makes my kind of ham roll—one that's hot with gooey melted cheese and mustard butter inside.

MAKES 24 PARTY-SIZED ROLLS OR 12 DINNER ROLLS

24 party rolls or 12 dinner rolls
1 tablespoon unsalted butter
1/2 medium yellow onion, sliced thin
1/2 teaspoon dried thyme
1 stick unsalted butter, softened
3 tablespoons spicy brown mustard
1 teaspoon Worcestershire sauce
1/4 teaspoon Tabasco sauce
1/2 pound good-quality Virginia baked ham, sliced very thin
1/3 pound swiss cheese, sliced very thin

Use rolls that are connected together in sheets of 6 dinner rolls or 12 party rolls, with 2 sheets per package. Cut both sheets of rolls in half horizontally, creating a top and bottom layer.

In a small saucepan over medium heat, melt the tablespoon of butter. Add the onions and thyme and cook for 2–3 minutes, just until the onions start to soften. Remove from heat.

In a small bowl, add the stick of softened butter, mustard, Worcestershire, and Tabasco. Stir together until a smooth and creamy spread has formed.

Spread the mustard and butter mixture evenly over each cut side of the rolls. Place an even layer of ham on the bottom half of the rolls. On top of the ham, spread an even layer of onions. On top of the onions, add an even layer of swiss cheese. Place the top layer of the rolls on the cheese, onion, and ham layers. Wrap each sheet of 6 or 12 rolls separately in a layer of aluminum foil and refrigerate overnight. Transport to your tailgate in a cooler.

Prior to serving, place the foil-wrapped rolls on a medium-high grill for 5–10 minutes, until the cheese and butter melts. Flip the rolls halfway through. Once cooked, remove from the grill and let cool for a minute. Cut the rolls apart before serving.

Onion Rings and Fried Pickles

Some people like onion rings. Some people like fried pickles. Rather than choose, I suggest making both. The dredge can be used on both pickles and onions. The pickles are washed in a mixture containing pickle juice, and the onion rings are dipped in a wash containing apple cider vinegar.

MAKES 8 SERVINGS

4 large yellow onions
1 (24-ounce) jar of pickle spears

Dredge
2 cups self-rising flour
2 cups self-rising white cornmeal
2 teaspoons black pepper
2 teaspoons salt
2 teaspoons paprika
$\frac{1}{2}$ teaspoon cayenne pepper

Onion Wash
2 cups 2 percent milk
2 eggs, lightly beaten
1 tablespoon apple cider vinegar

Pickle Wash
2 cups 2 percent milk
2 eggs, lightly beaten
1 tablespoon pickle juice

The night before the tailgate, measure out the flour, cornmeal, black pepper, salt, paprika, and cayenne pepper. Pack in a sealable container.

For the onion ring wash, add the milk, eggs, and vinegar to a sealable container. For the pickle wash, add the milk, eggs, and pickle juice to a sealable container. Store the sealable containers of wash in the refrigerator overnight and transport in a cooler to your tailgate.

At the tailgate, prepare the onions and pickles. Slice the onions into rings and add the rings to a container of ice water. Let the rings soak in the ice water for 10 minutes. Remove and pat dry. Remove the pickles from the jar and pat dry.

Place the onions and pickles into the dredge mixture and stir to cover completely. Remove from the dredge and place in the appropriate wash. Transfer from the wash back to the dredge, coating completely. Fry in 365–370° oil for 1–2 minutes, until golden brown. Fry in small batches to prevent the oil temperature from changing too drastically. Once done, remove from the oil and drain on a tray lined with paper bags.

Onion Rings

Pepperoni Rolls

In Morgantown, West Virginia, I came across a group of tailgaters with a tub filled with rolls. I walked over to the next tailgate and saw a similar tub of rolls. After a third sighting, I learned about the history of the West Virginia pepperoni roll and its coal-mining roots.

When miners are inside the mine for the entire day, they require a lunch that won't spoil. The pepperoni roll fits this niche and also turns out to be a great tailgating snack. The traditional roll is a soft, slightly sweet dough stuffed with a few pepperoni slices and then baked. Grease from the pepperoni leaks out onto the edges of the roll, leaving orange markings. I've heard from Mountaineer fans that the rolls are also great stuffed with pepperoni and cheese and dipped in marinara sauce. These rolls are easy to prepare the night before and can feed a crowd.

MAKES ABOUT 24 ROLLS

3 pounds of frozen dinner roll dough
1 (8-ounce) package of pepperoni slices
4 tablespoons unsalted butter, melted

Preheat the oven to 350°.

Let the frozen dough come to room temperature and divide into 24 pieces.

Form the dough into a flat circle about the size of your palm. Place 3 or 4 slices of pepperoni in the center. Fold the circle in half, pinch the edges together, and tuck the edges under the roll, creating an oval shape with the pepperoni sealed inside. Repeat until all the dough is used.

Place the rolls, pinched edges down, on a lined baking sheet. Brush the surface with melted butter. Bake for 15–20 minutes, until golden brown. Let cool and store in a sealable container overnight. At your tailgate, set out upon arrival.

Pepperoni Rolls

Sides provide the color and flavor that make a tailgating meal complete. They vary from fruit- or vegetable-based salads that take advantage of local produce to breads that are ideal for soaking up the sauce from main dishes. When you're a guest at a tailgate, it's a nice gesture to bring one of these sides as your contribution to the meal.

Sides

New Potato Salad

A potato salad with a refreshing vinaigrette is a great side for early-season tailgates. It's a satisfying dish that holds up well in the heat. I enjoy it on a plate next to Garlic-Rosemary Pork Tenderloin (page 133).

MAKES 10–12 SERVINGS

3 pounds new potatoes, skin on, rinsed well
2 teaspoons salt
1 garlic clove
1 1/2 teaspoons Dijon mustard
1 tablespoon dill pickle juice
4 teaspoons apple cider vinegar
1 teaspoon sugar
1/4 teaspoon Tabasco sauce
1/2 teaspoon salt
1/4 teaspoon McCormick Coarse Ground Black Pepper
1/2 cup corn oil
1 cup chopped celery
1/2 cup chopped flat-leaf parsley
1/2 cup grated carrots
1/3 cup dill pickle chips, diced
1/4 cup chopped scallions (white and green parts)
2 tablespoons finely chopped shallots

In a large pot, add the potatoes. Add water until the potatoes are just covered and bring to a boil. Add the salt. Cook the potatoes until fork tender. Drain and let cool. Cover the top of the pot with a paper towel or a clean dishcloth.

While the potatoes are cooling, make the vinaigrette. Place the garlic, mustard, pickle juice, vinegar, sugar, Tabasco, salt, and pepper in the bowl of a food processor. Turn the food processor on and, as it mixes, slowly drizzle the oil into the bowl in a steady stream. Set the vinaigrette aside.

Quarter the cooled potatoes and transfer them to a large bowl. Add the celery, parsley, carrots, pickles, scallions, and shallots. Toss together.

Pour the vinaigrette over the potatoes and vegetables and toss together. Store in a sealable container and refrigerate overnight. On game day, transport to your tailgate in a cooler. Toss before serving.

Roasted Sweet Potato Salad (p. 92) and New Potato Salad

Roasted Sweet Potato Salad

If your tailgating table is decked out in orange on game days, wouldn't it make sense to serve a potato salad to match? Sweet potatoes are a fantastic option for a cold salad. Their vibrant orange color and sweeter flavor make for a different twist on traditional potato salad.

MAKES 10–12 SERVINGS

10 cups peeled sweet potatoes, cut into bite-sized pieces

3 tablespoons olive oil

1 teaspoon salt

1 teaspoon black pepper

2 cups fresh pineapple, cut into bite-sized pieces

¾ cup diced red bell peppers

¾ cup diced yellow bell peppers

½ cup finely chopped shallots

1 jalapeño, seeded and finely chopped

½ cup chopped cilantro leaves

½ cup chopped flat-leaf parsley

¼ cup chopped scallions

2 tablespoons apple cider vinegar

2 tablespoons brown sugar

2 teaspoons grated orange zest

1 teaspoon deli-style mustard

¼ teaspoon salt

½ cup corn oil

Preheat the oven to 425°.

In a medium-sized bowl, toss the sweet potatoes with the olive oil, salt, and pepper. Spread in a single layer on a nonstick baking sheet. Roast, stirring every 5 minutes, until fork tender and slightly browned on the edges, about 25–30 minutes. Remove from the oven and let cool.

In a large bowl, add the pineapple, peppers, shallots, jalapeño, cilantro, parsley, scallions, and cooled sweet potatoes.

In a small bowl, prepare the vinaigrette. Add the vinegar, brown sugar, orange zest, mustard, and salt. Whisk continuously while slowly pouring in the oil. Whisk until all the ingredients are incorporated.

Pour the dressing over the sweet potato salad and toss. Chill in the refrigerator overnight. On game day, transport to your tailgate in a cooler and keep covered until ready to serve. Toss again prior to serving.

Broccoli Salad

Looking for something a little different to bring to your tailgate? Try Broccoli Salad. With a subtle, creamy orange dressing, this light and crunchy side is an unusual and delicious supplement to a tailgating menu. Baylor, USF, and William and Mary fans will find that the green and gold complement the colors on their tailgating tables.

MAKES 10–12 SERVINGS

10 cups broccoli florets, chopped into bite-sized pieces
8 slices of bacon, cooked and crumbled
¼ cup chopped shallots
¼ cup chopped red onions
½ cup golden raisins
½ cup chopped apricots
½ cup shelled sunflower seeds
1 cup mayonnaise
¼ cup fresh orange juice
2 tablespoons apple cider vinegar
2 tablespoons sugar
2 teaspoons grated orange zest

In a large bowl, add the broccoli, bacon, shallots, onion, raisins, apricots, and sunflower seeds. In a small bowl, add the rest of the ingredients and whisk together, forming a creamy dressing. Pour the dressing over the broccoli salad and toss. Store refrigerated in a sealable container overnight. On game day, keep in a cooler until ready to serve. Toss before serving.

Carrot-Raisin Salad

If you're an Auburn or Oklahoma State fan, or the fan of any other orange school, you don't want to serve the same orange foods every week. Try this refreshing Carrot-Raisin Salad. Its crunchy texture and bright citrus and ginger flavors work on their own or as a topping for Teriyaki Pork Tenderloin (page 132) or chicken sandwiches.

MAKES 8 SERVINGS

8 cups grated carrots
¾ cup dark raisins
¼ cup dark brown sugar
2 tablespoons corn oil
2 tablespoons fresh orange juice
1 tablespoon fresh lemon juice
½ teaspoon salt
½ teaspoon grated orange zest
½ teaspoon grated lemon zest
¼ teaspoon peeled and grated fresh ginger

Place the carrots in a large bowl. Add the raisins and stir. In a separate bowl, add the rest of the ingredients and stir. Pour over the carrot salad and toss. Refrigerate in a sealable serving container. Transport in a cooler on game day and toss before serving.

Zesty Arugula and Kale Salad (p. 96),
Carrot-Raisin Salad, and Broccoli Salad (p. 93)

Zesty Arugula and Kale Salad

With its clean taste and beautiful green color, this salad adds balance to heavy and rich tailgating food. Quick and easy to prepare, it's an ideal side salad for the main meal. Zesty Arugula and Kale Salad can also be used to top a wide variety of sandwiches.

MAKES 8–10 SERVINGS

5 cups baby arugula, loosely packed
4 cups baby kale, torn into bite-sized pieces and loosely packed
1 cup chopped mint leaves
3 tablespoons extra-virgin olive oil
1 tablespoon balsamic vinegar
1 teaspoon grated lemon zest
$\frac{1}{8}$ teaspoon salt
$\frac{1}{8}$ teaspoon black pepper

The morning of the tailgate, wash the arugula, kale, and mint. Dry in a salad spinner. Empty the salad onto a double layer of paper towels. Loosely wrap in the paper towels and store in a sealable plastic bag. Refrigerate until leaving for the tailgate and transport in a cooler.

In a small sealable container, combine the rest of the ingredients. At the tailgate, vigorously shake the dressing. Toss the salad in a large serving bowl. Pour the dressing over the salad and toss again until it's coated in dressing. Serve immediately.

Fruit Cups with
Sour Cream and Yogurt Dressing

Do your tailgating guests prefer a lighter side dish during their pregame brunch? A fruit cup will deliver the color and sweetness you may be seeking. Melons, berries, grapes, or even peeled citrus slices—a wide variety of seasonal fruits will work. Serving the fruit in a large bowl allows guests to help themselves. Finish this fruit cup by topping it with a creamy sour cream and yogurt dressing.

MAKES 8 SERVINGS

8 cups assorted fresh fruit, cut into bite-sized pieces
1 cup nonfat vanilla yogurt
1 cup sour cream
2 tablespoons dark brown sugar
1 teaspoon grated orange zest
1/8 teaspoon freshly grated nutmeg

In a large sealable container, mix together the assorted fruit. Cover and refrigerate overnight.

In a medium-sized bowl, add the rest of the ingredients and mix until smooth. Refrigerate overnight.

On game day, transport the fruit and yogurt sauce in a cooler. Dress the fruit when serving. You can either put the salad in cups before your guests arrive or allow them to make their own cups.

Blistered Grape Tomatoes

Blistered Grape Tomatoes

Marinating tomatoes and onions in seasonings and then roasting them in a pan over the grill is a quick way to create a condiment that can be used in a variety of other dishes. Cooking this dish allows for some showmanship and flair, which will make it a signature dish at your tailgate.

MAKES 8 SERVINGS

4 pints grape tomatoes (red and yellow)
1 medium yellow onion, thinly sliced
1/3 cup olive oil
1 tablespoon balsamic vinegar
1/2 teaspoon salt
1/4 teaspoon McCormick Coarse Ground Black Pepper
1/4 teaspoon oregano
1/4 teaspoon cumin

The night before the tailgate, place the tomatoes and onions in a sealable plastic bag. In a smaller bowl, whisk together the rest of the ingredients. Pour the marinade into the bag of tomatoes and onions. Seal and refrigerate overnight. Transport in a cooler to your tailgate.

At your tailgate, you'll need a sheet pan, roasting pan, or some other grill-proof container large enough to accommodate the tomatoes spread out in a single layer. Place the pan with the tomatoes over a medium-high grill. Cook, stirring frequently, until the tomatoes begin to blister. Transfer to an aluminum roasting pan or other serving container. Serve warm or at room temperature.

Grilled Fruit Platter

Wow your guests with a memorable Grilled Fruit Platter. A grilled fruit display is a delicious, healthy, and refreshing option for your guests. You can use a wide variety of fruits.

MAKES 8–12 SERVINGS

Assorted seasonal fruit (pineapple, watermelon,
   pears, plums, peaches, apples, nectarines),
   cut into uniform-sized pieces
1 cup apple juice
½ cup pineapple juice
3 tablespoons honey
3 tablespoons fresh lime juice
¼ teaspoon salt
2 tablespoons corn oil

The night before the tailgate, wash and cut the fruit and pack in a sealable plastic bag.

Pour the apple juice and pineapple juice into a high-sided saucepan. Bring to a boil over medium-high heat. Boil for 10 minutes until the liquid is reduced by half. Remove from heat and cool for 10 minutes. Add the honey and stir. Add the lime juice and salt and stir. Add the corn oil. Pour the liquid into a sealable container. Refrigerate the fruit and the juice mixture overnight and transport to the tailgate in a cooler.

At the tailgate, shake the grilling sauce vigorously. Pour half over the fruit and toss. Grill the fruit over a medium-high grill on both sides until grilling marks have formed. Softer fruits like watermelon and plums will take less time to grill than harder fruits like pears and apples. Baste with additional grilling sauce. Serve the grilled fruit on a large platter or sheet pan.

Grilled Fruit Platter

Tailgating with Local Ingredients

Many tailgaters take pride in sourcing their game-day spreads from the fields, forests, and bodies of water closest to their homes. Whether it's the protein for the main dish or the vegetables and fruits for a side, a number of tailgaters prefer to serve food grown close to them.

College football tailgating season coincides with hunting season. This provides no shortage of game birds and venison in game-day tailgating spreads. For example, Texas fan Samantha Fechtel likes to grill quail or dove wrapped in cream cheese, bacon, and jalapeño. I've seen plenty of tailgaters who use the game they catch as part of their game-day spread.

On campuses close to the coast, an abundance of fresh seafood can be found. In Greenville, North Carolina, I met a group of tailgaters who had palm-sized oysters they had picked up that morning straight from the North Carolina coast. In Raleigh, a North Carolina State fan from Emerald Isle had brought fresh blue crabs for his crab boil. In Baton Rouge, I met a

tailgater whose locally sourced crabs were from nearby Lake Pontchartrain. Seafood wasn't the only freshly caught item I saw at LSU. At a large tailgate in the RV lot, I came across one tailgater by the name of Dynamite who was frying up frog legs and alligator tail. While

Boiled peanuts on sale at the Florida versus Georgia game in Jacksonville

sampling his dishes, I learned that Dynamite had caught both of the items himself.

While a story about growing your own produce isn't as entertaining as one about catching your own alligator, vegetables are the most abundant local items on tailgaters' menus. From sweet potatoes in the sweet potato salad to the finely shredded cabbage in the slaw, tailgaters from all over the South bring the best of their local produce with them on game day. Some bring vegetables picked from their gardens the day before. Others purchase produce from a midweek farmers' market.

As late summer turns into fall and fall into winter, the produce that tailgaters bring with them changes too. The watermelon that you see on a hot Labor Day weekend kickoff game is replaced by greens and pumpkins at the end of the season. And, as tailgaters travel to other campuses, they take advantage of southern delicacies that might not be available in their regions. The product of southern peanut growers can be seen at tailgates throughout Florida, Georgia, and South Carolina. Some tailgaters may make their own boiled peanuts, but it's more common for them to be seen for sale in stands around the stadiums, having been boiled in enormous pots throughout the day. For a dollar a bag, tailgaters can enjoy this unique snack as they walk around and visit friends.

The change from warmer to cooler game days doesn't mean you have to forgo the delicious produce you enjoyed earlier in the summer. Canned and preserved produce is common at many tailgates. By serving canned or pickled produce, cruets of hot pepper vinegars, and jars of jams and preserves, tailgaters can invite their guests to enjoy the flavors of the summer all year round. ■

Apple-Pecan Chicken Salad

Chicken salad is always a crowd-pleaser; it can be eaten between two slices of grilled bread as a sandwich or as a side on your plate. If you like chicken salad, give this one a try.

MAKES 8 SERVINGS

3 tablespoons lemon juice

1½ cups chopped red apples, skin on

8 cups chopped cooked chicken

1½ cups chopped celery

1¼ cups chopped, toasted pecans

1¼ cups mayonnaise

⅓ cup apple juice

1 tablespoon Worcestershire sauce

1 teaspoon salt

½ teaspoon Tabasco sauce

¼ teaspoon McCormick Coarse Ground Black Pepper

In a small bowl, combine the lemon juice and chopped apples. In a large bowl, combine the chicken, celery, and pecans. Add the lemon-soaked apples to the large bowl.

In a medium-sized bowl, combine the mayonnaise, apple juice, Worcestershire, salt, Tabasco, and pepper. Stir. Pour the dressing over the chicken, celery, pecans, and apples. Mix until the ingredients are evenly coated with the dressing. Store in a sealable container and refrigerate overnight. On game day, keep this dish in a cooler until you're ready to eat.

Apple-Pecan Chicken Salad, Curried Chicken Salad (p. 104), and Smoked Turkey Salad (p. 105)

Curried Chicken Salad

This curried chicken salad is a standout. Its golden color is studded with almonds, grapes, raisins, and peaches. Try it. It may become your new favorite.

MAKES 8 SERVINGS

8 cups chopped cooked chicken breast
1½ cups chopped celery
1½ cups slivered almonds, toasted
1 cup quartered seedless green grapes
1 cup yellow raisins
2 tablespoons finely chopped shallots
1 (15¼-ounce) can of peaches in heavy syrup,
    drained and chopped, syrup reserved
1 cup mayonnaise
2 tablespoons curry powder
1 tablespoon lemon juice
4 teaspoons dark brown sugar
1 teaspoon Worcestershire sauce
1 teaspoon grated lemon zest
1 teaspoon grated orange zest
1 teaspoon salt
¼ teaspoon Tabasco sauce
¼ teaspoon McCormick Coarse Ground Black Pepper

In a large bowl, add the chicken, celery, almonds, grapes, raisins, and shallots. Toss together. In a medium-sized bowl, mix together the rest of the ingredients. Pour over the chicken mixture. Stir until all the ingredients are evenly mixed. Store in a sealable container and refrigerate overnight. On game day, keep in a cooler until you're ready to eat.

Smoked Turkey Salad

During the latter part of the season, turkey is the bird on everyone's mind. This turkey salad is filled with fall flavors ideal for sandwiches or for eating with crackers as a side. It's best when made with Dry-Brined Turkey Breast (page 149), but if you have abundant amounts of leftover Thanksgiving turkey, feel free to use it in this recipe.

MAKES 8 SERVINGS

8 cups smoked turkey breast, cut into bite-sized cubes
1 ¼ cups dried cranberries
1 ¼ cups chopped celery
1 (6-ounce) package of shelled, roasted, and salted pistachios
¼ cup finely chopped shallots
2 cups mayonnaise
¼ cup chopped parsley
4 tablespoons lime juice
1 teaspoon grated lime zest
¼ teaspoon salt
¼ teaspoon McCormick Coarse Ground Black Pepper

In a large bowl, add the turkey, cranberries, celery, pistachios, and shallots. Toss together. In a medium-sized bowl, whisk together the rest of the ingredients until a smooth and creamy dressing is created. Pour over the turkey mixture. Toss until all the salad ingredients are evenly coated by the dressing. Transfer to a sealable container and refrigerate. Transport to your tailgate in a cooler and remove when you're ready to serve. Stir before serving.

Tailgating Tent Cities

An essential piece of tailgating equipment is the 10 × 10-foot pop-up canopy tent. These tents provide shade when it's hot, keep you dry when it's wet, and, when sides are added, block the cold wind of late-season games. They come in a wide range of colors, which makes them perfect for showing allegiance to your team. As versatile as they are, it's no surprise that on game days, these tents cover all available green space on campuses across the South.

These tent cities spring up overnight, only to vanish the next day. Tent cities can number anywhere from a half-dozen tents scattered around a lawn to dozens of interconnected tents. Every school has its own version of a tent city.

Circle Park in Knoxville, the Amphitheater in Auburn, the Plaza of the Americas in Gainesville, and Myers Quad in Athens are all areas that serve two purposes. On weekdays, they are used by students as commuter paths or as areas to toss a football or study. On game days, these areas transform into tent cities filled with hundreds of tailgaters. On a few campuses, these tent cities are the epicenter of tailgating on campus. When thousands of tailgaters centralize their pregame festivities in one location, these tent cities become something truly spectacular.

Ole Miss: The Grove

Your first trip to the Grove at Ole Miss is something you'll never forget. It's an atmosphere and place unlike any other. On game day eve, fans line up around the Grove waiting for it to open so they can claim their tailgating spot and set up their tent for the next day's game. Overnight, this tranquil, ten-acre green space transforms into a sea of red, white, and blue tents. If it wasn't for the spray-painted blue lines and brick-lined Walk of Champions creating pathways, the entire ten acres would be one large, connected tent.

A Saturday in the Grove is more than just a tailgate. These Ole Miss home games are the social events of the season. Women wear heels and their finest sundresses. Men wear seersucker suits and bow ties. Tailgating in the Grove is a chance for friends, families, undergrads, and alums to see and be seen. Fine linens and silver serving dishes cover many of the tables, so the decor is more like what you would find at a cocktail party than what you might traditionally expect at a tailgate. Don't be fooled, though; there's still a football game and plenty of team spirit. About two and a half hours before kickoff, the players walk single-file down the Walk of Champions toward the stadium.

Alabama: The Quad

The place to congregate in Tuscaloosa on game day is a large grass quadrangle a block from Bryant-Denny Stadium. Most of the more than 100,000 fans who come to every Alabama home game will pass through the Quad. Whether hosting a tailgate, seeing the handprints of former players at the base of the bell tower known as Denny Chimes, or visiting a friend's tailgate on the way to the game, fans know the Quad as the center of all tailgating activity. Tailgaters can claim their spot and set up a tent the night before, so the Quad is open for a full day of tailgating on game day. Tailgating activity is in full swing until about an hour before kickoff, when the band holds a pregame performance known as the "Elephant Stomp" on the steps of Gorgas Library. The Million Dollar Band fires up the crowd as they lead the march to the stadium for kickoff. Whether it's your first tailgate or your hundredth, tailgating in the Quad is the quintessential way to experience game day in Tuscaloosa.

Mississippi State: The Junction

On game days in Starkville, Mississippi, over 55,000 fans fill Davis Wade Stadium. Before the game, these fans tailgate on the MSU campus in an area known as "the Junction." The Junction has evolved from an intersection of rail lines into a five-way street intersection once nicknamed "Malfunction Junction" to its current iteration, a public green space with bronze bulldog statues at two of the entrances.

The Junction is filled with spirit on game day. Be sure to witness the pregame player procession known as the "Dawg Walk." Hundreds of fans will line the path, ringing their cowbells and cheering. The Junction opens for a few hours the night before the game for fans to claim their spots and set up their tents for the next day's tailgates. When you're in Starkville for a game, you and your cowbell should "Hail State" at the Junction.

Southern Methodist University: The Boulevard

I was once told by an SMU fan that he doesn't tailgate, he "Boulevards." Game-day festivities at SMU are held in a grassy area on campus known as "the Boulevard." Shortly after the opening of Gerald J. Ford Stadium brought football back to the SMU campus, the Boulevard quickly became the central gathering place for SMU tailgating. Along the picturesque, tree-lined Bishop Boulevard, thousands of fans will gather under an array of red, white, and blue tents. With live music and delicious tailgating spreads, fans of all ages will have a blast "Boulevarding" before SMU takes the field. ■

Tailgaters in The Grove at Ole Miss

Pasta Salad

Tailgates tend to be meat-centric events, but you may have guests who live a vegetarian lifestyle. They'll appreciate seeing this pasta salad. Be careful, though—once they've tasted it, there's a good chance that even the fiercest carnivores at the tailgate will have a pile of it on their plate.

MAKES 8 SERVINGS

$\frac{1}{3}$ cup red wine vinegar
1 tablespoon Dijon mustard
1 tablespoon chopped garlic
$\frac{3}{4}$ teaspoon salt
$\frac{1}{4}$ teaspoon McCormick Coarse Ground Black Pepper
1 cup extra-virgin olive oil
1 pound mini penne pasta (or pasta of your choice)
2 pints red grape tomatoes
$\frac{1}{3}$ cup finely chopped shallots
2 tablespoons olive oil
$\frac{2}{3}$ cup diced red bell peppers
$\frac{2}{3}$ cup diced yellow bell peppers
$\frac{2}{3}$ cup diced green bell peppers
$\frac{1}{3}$ cup diced poblano peppers
$1\frac{1}{2}$ cups Parmesan cheese
8 ounces Gouda cheese, cut into bite-sized cubes
$\frac{1}{3}$ cup snipped chives
$\frac{1}{3}$ cup chopped scallions (white and green parts)

Start by making the vinaigrette. In the bowl of a food processor, add the vinegar, mustard, garlic, salt, and pepper. Process until blended. With the processor still running, add the extra-virgin olive oil in a slow and steady stream. When all the oil is absorbed, turn the processor off and set the vinaigrette aside.

In a large pot of boiling salted water, cook the pasta for 7–10 minutes until just al dente. Drain and place in a large bowl. Toss the warm pasta with the vinaigrette and set aside.

In a medium-sized nonstick saucepan, add the tomatoes, shallots, and 2 tablespoons olive oil. Cook over medium-high heat, stirring frequently for 3–5 minutes, until the tomatoes have begun to blister. Remove from heat and pour over the cooked pasta.

Add the peppers to the cooked pasta and stir. Add the Parmesan cheese and stir until the pasta is evenly coated. Add the Gouda, chives, and scallions. Toss until all the ingredients are evenly mixed. Store in a sealable container and refrigerate overnight. Transfer in a cooler to your tailgate.

Tailgating Beans

If you're the type of tailgater who arrives at a tailgate many hours before kickoff, you know that good things are worth the wait. For this recipe, dried beans are soaked the night before and transformed into something special with a little patience and a lot of stirring. With the first bite, you'll understand that cooking beans low and slow over an open flame is the way to go.

MAKES 10–12 SERVINGS

2 pounds dry navy beans

4 tablespoons bacon drippings

2 cups chopped yellow onions

1 cup chopped green bell peppers

$\frac{1}{4}$ cup chopped and seeded jalapeño peppers

1 tablespoon chopped garlic

$\frac{1}{2}$ cup dark brown sugar

$\frac{1}{2}$ cup unsulphured molasses (like Grandma's Original)

$\frac{1}{2}$ cup ketchup

$\frac{1}{3}$ cup brown deli-style mustard

1 tablespoon paprika

2 teaspoons chili powder

$\frac{1}{2}$ teaspoon black pepper

$\frac{1}{4}$ teaspoon cayenne pepper

2 teaspoons salt

2 (32-ounce) boxes of low-sodium chicken stock

The night before the tailgate, place the navy beans in enough water to cover the beans by 4 inches and soak overnight. Drain the beans and remove any debris. Place the beans in a sealable container and refrigerate overnight. Pack the bacon drippings in a sealable container. Pack the onions, peppers, and garlic in a sealable container and refrigerate overnight. Pack the dark brown sugar, molasses, ketchup, and mustard in a sealable container. Pack the paprika, chili powder, black pepper, and cayenne pepper in a sealable container. Pack the salt separately since it will be added at the end of cooking. Transport the refrigerated containers in a cooler to your tailgate.

The beans will be cooked using a propane burner. In a high-sided stockpot over medium heat, melt the bacon drippings. Add the onions, peppers, and garlic. Stir and cook for about 5 minutes, until the onions are translucent and the peppers soften.

Add the beans and the chicken stock and bring to a boil. Reduce heat to a simmer and cover. Simmer for 2–2½ hours, stirring every 15 minutes. Remove the lid, add the dark brown sugar and molasses mixture, and stir. Add the spice mixture and stir. Simmer uncovered for 45 minutes. Add the salt, stir, and turn the beans to low until ready to serve.

Deviled Eggs

Deviled eggs are like Bloody Marys—you either love them or you stay away from them. They both can be topped with an assortment of garnishes or consumed plain. Everyone has an opinion on what they should or shouldn't be. This is how my mom likes her deviled eggs—with a creamy center, firm white, and no garnish.

MAKES 24 DEVILED EGGS

12 hard-boiled eggs, peeled
¾ cup mayonnaise
2 teaspoons Creole mustard
1 teaspoon sugar
¼ teaspoon salt
¼ teaspoon Tabasco sauce

Cut the eggs in half lengthwise and remove the cooked yolks. Place the yolks in the bowl of a food processor and set the egg white halves aside.

Add the mayonnaise, mustard, sugar, salt, and Tabasco to the bowl. Pulse until a smooth filling has formed. Using either a spoon or a piping bag, fill the egg white halves with the yolk mixture. Place in a sealable container and refrigerate overnight. On the day of the tailgate, transport to the game in a cooler.

Deviled Eggs

Confetti Slaw

At the end of the season, every tailgater wants his or her team to be the one showered by confetti after a national championship win. This crunchy and colorful slaw is a good reminder of that sight. It combines the bright colors of assorted peppers with shredded green and purple cabbage, all mixed together in a vinegar-based dressing. This is a side that will go with any main entrée.

MAKES 8 SERVINGS

1 cup English cucumbers, halved lengthwise and sliced thin

6 cups green cabbage, cut into long, thin strips

3 cups red cabbage, cut into long, thin strips

½ cup diced red bell peppers

½ cup diced orange bell peppers

½ cup diced yellow bell peppers

3 tablespoons chopped parsley

1 tablespoon finely chopped shallots

1 tablespoon snipped chives

½ cup apple cider vinegar

2 tablespoons light brown sugar

1 teaspoon salt

¼ teaspoon McCormick Coarse Ground Black Pepper

In a large bowl, mix together the cucumbers, cabbages, peppers, parsley, shallots, and chives. In a small bowl, whisk together the rest of the ingredients until the sugar has completely dissolved.

Pour the dressing over the slaw and toss, making sure to evenly coat all the slaw. Store in a sealable bag or container and refrigerate overnight. Transport to your tailgate in a cooler. Toss again prior to serving.

Creamy Coleslaw

When barbecue is dressed with a strong and tangy vinegar-based sauce, you'll find that nothing complements the dish better than coleslaw. The creamy texture and slightly sweet flavor cuts through the bite of the vinegar. This slaw isn't just for barbecue, though. It pairs well with any spicy food or can be used as a topping on chili dogs or sandwiches.

MAKES 8 SERVINGS

1 large head of cabbage
1 bread-and-butter pickle spear
¾ cup mayonnaise
3 tablespoons white vinegar
3 tablespoons sugar
1 tablespoon bread-and-butter pickle juice
½ teaspoon salt
⅛ teaspoon white pepper

Cut the cabbage into large pieces. Add the cabbage and pickle spear to the bowl of a food processor and process until the cabbage is coarsely chopped. You'll need enough cabbage to yield 8 cups. Place the cabbage and pickle in a large bowl.

In a medium-sized bowl, add the rest of the ingredients. Whisk together, creating a smooth dressing. Pour the dressing over the slaw and stir until all the slaw has been evenly coated with the dressing. Store in a sealable container and refrigerate overnight. On game day, store in a cooler until ready to eat.

Hushpuppies

Hushpuppies are amazing. Hot from the fryer and served with butter, they are irresistible. If your team is playing a school with a dog as a mascot, silence the competition and eat them at the same time.

MAKES 10–12 SERVINGS

2½ cups self-rising white cornmeal
¼ cup self-rising flour
1 tablespoon sugar
1¼ cups buttermilk
¼ cup finely grated yellow onions
¼ cup corn oil
1 egg, beaten
Peanut oil for frying

The night before the game, pack the cornmeal, flour, and sugar in a sealable container. Place the buttermilk, onions, corn oil, and egg in a sealable container, refrigerate it overnight, and transport it to the tailgate in a cooler.

At the tailgate, add the flour mixture to a bowl and stir. Pour the buttermilk and egg mixture into the bowl and stir, creating a thick batter. Let the batter rest for 15–20 minutes. Meanwhile, heat the frying oil to 370°.

Once the oil has heated and the batter has rested, dip a metal spoon into the batter and scoop out ping-pong-ball-sized hushpuppies. Use a second spoon to scrape the balls of batter off the first spoon and into the oil. Let fry until golden brown on both sides, flipping halfway through. Remove from the oil and place on a paper bag–lined tray to drain.

Hushpuppies

Scallion, White Cheddar, and Ham Cornbread

Try this savory twist on traditional cornbread. It goes great with soups, stews, salads, and items from the grill. It can also stand alone when warmed on the grill and served with butter.

MAKES 8 SERVINGS

2 tablespoons bacon drippings

4 tablespoons unsalted butter

1½ cups plain yellow cornmeal

1½ cups grated white cheddar cheese

½ cup all-purpose flour

½ cup chopped scallions (white and green parts)

2 tablespoons snipped chives

1 tablespoon baking powder

2 teaspoons sugar

1 teaspoon baking soda

¼ teaspoon salt

½ cup chopped thinly sliced dry-cured ham

2 tablespoons diced onions

2 large eggs, beaten

1¼ cups buttermilk

¼ teaspoon Tabasco sauce

Preheat the oven to 400°.

Place the bacon drippings and butter in a seasoned 12-inch cast-iron skillet. Place the skillet in the oven until the drippings and butter are melted.

Meanwhile, combine the cornmeal, cheddar cheese, flour, scallions, chives, baking powder, sugar, baking soda, and salt in a large bowl. Mix together.

In a small saucepan, cook the chopped ham and onions for 2–3 minutes over medium-low heat, until the onions start to soften. Remove from heat.

In a small bowl, combine the eggs, buttermilk, and Tabasco. Add the cooked ham and onions and mix together. Carefully remove the hot skillet from the oven. Pour the melted bacon drippings and butter into the egg and buttermilk mixture and stir. Quickly pour the wet ingredients into the dry ingredients and stir with a fork just until a smooth batter forms.

Pour the batter into the hot skillet and return it to the oven. Bake for 20–25 minutes. Let the cornbread cool. Remove from the pan and wrap tightly in aluminum foil. Set out at the beginning of the tailgate on game day. Slice into wedges prior to serving.

Sharp Cheddar Beer Bread

Taking a note from my mom, I adapted her beer bread to fit my college experience. Living in Madison, I had an abundance of Wisconsin cheese on hand. Naturally, it made its way into Sharp Cheddar Beer Bread. Adding a slice of cheddar cheese on top and grilling turns this into delicious cheese toast.

MAKES 8 SERVINGS

2 cups self-rising flour
1 1/2 cups grated sharp cheddar cheese
1 cup self-rising yellow cornmeal
1/3 cup sugar
1/2 teaspoon paprika
1/4 teaspoon cayenne pepper
1 (12-ounce) bottle of your favorite IPA or pilsner beer
1 stick unsalted butter, melted

Preheat the oven to 350°.

In a medium-sized bowl, add the flour, cheese, cornmeal, sugar, paprika, and cayenne pepper. Stir. Pour in the bottle of beer and stir until a batter forms. Pour the batter into a greased 9 × 5-inch metal loaf pan and spread it out evenly. Pour the melted butter over the top of the batter. Bake for 40–45 minutes, until a tester comes out clean. Remove from the pan and let cool. Wrap in aluminum foil and transport to your tailgate. Serve plain or buttered and grilled at your tailgate.

Poppy Seed–Pale Ale Beer Bread

Poppy Seed–Pale Ale Beer Bread

There are few foods that say "college" like beer bread. It's inexpensive to make and will fill you up. My mom lived on the stuff during her undergraduate years at Duke and in law school at UNC. During late-night study sessions, Poppy Seed–Pale Ale Beer Bread was her go-to study-break snack.

MAKES 8 SERVINGS

2 cups self-rising flour
1 cup self-rising white cornmeal
⅓ cup sugar
1 tablespoon poppy seeds plus 1 teaspoon
1 (12-ounce) bottle of your favorite pale ale
1 stick unsalted butter, melted

Preheat the oven to 350°.

In a medium-sized bowl, combine the flour, cornmeal, sugar, and 1 tablespoon of the poppy seeds. Stir, mixing the ingredients evenly. Add the bottle of beer. Stir, creating a thick batter. Pour the batter into a greased 9 × 5-inch metal loaf pan and spread into an even layer. Sprinkle the top with the remaining 1 teaspoon of poppy seeds. Pour the melted butter on top. Bake for 40–45 minutes, until a tester comes out clean. Remove from the pan and let cool. Wrap in aluminum foil and transport to your tailgate.

Spiced Pumpkin Beer Bread

When football season is in full swing, craft breweries roll out their pumpkin beer. Our homage to this seasonal brew is Spiced Pumpkin Beer Bread, chock-full of raisins, dates, and spices. Try this as a side with a steaming bowl of Chow-Down Chili (page 160).

MAKES 8 SERVINGS

2 cups self-rising flour
1 cup self-rising yellow cornmeal
⅓ cup sugar
⅓ cup golden raisins
⅓ cup chopped dates
⅛ teaspoon freshly grated nutmeg
⅛ teaspoon ground cloves
⅓ cup pumpkin purée
1 (12-ounce) bottle of pumpkin ale
1 stick unsalted butter, melted

Preheat the oven to 350°.

In a medium-sized bowl, add the flour, cornmeal, sugar, raisins, dates, nutmeg, and cloves. Stir to mix the ingredients. Add the pumpkin and beer to a small bowl. Stir until mixed together. Pour the pumpkin-beer mixture into the flour mixture and stir until you create a thick batter. Pour into a greased 9 × 5-inch metal loaf pan and spread into an even layer. Pour the melted butter over the top. Bake for 40–45 minutes, until a tester comes out clean. Remove from the pan and let cool. Wrap in aluminum foil and transport to your tailgate.

Your tailgate will most likely center around one grilled, fried, or smoked item. This main entrée is the star of your parking lot party. It can be themed around your team or the competition or can simply be your favorite dish. Whether feeding a tailgate for two or for twenty, these main dishes will leave a lasting impression on your guests.

Main Meals

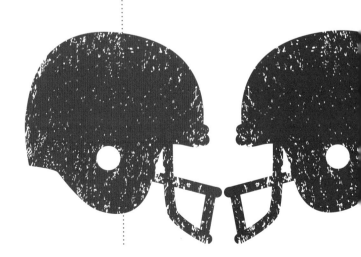

Steak and Creamer Potato Kabobs and
Chicken–Sweet Potato Kabobs (p. 124)

Steak and Creamer Potato Kabobs

This is a tailgating version of meat and potatoes. Not only are Steak and Creamer Potato Kabobs delicious, but, when served with Lemon-Scallion Rice (page 126) and a Zesty Arugula and Kale Salad (page 96), they're a complete meal.

MAKES 12 KABOBS

2 pounds sirloin steak, trimmed and cut into uniform,
   bite-sized cubes
3 green bell peppers
1 red onion
2 pounds Yukon Gold creamer potatoes, parboiled just until
   fork tender

Meat Marinade
1/3 cup balsamic vinegar
2 tablespoons Worcestershire sauce
1 tablespoon chopped garlic
1 teaspoon Creole mustard
3/4 teaspoon salt
1/2 teaspoon McCormick Coarse Ground Black Pepper
1/2 teaspoon thyme
1/2 cup olive oil

Vegetable Marinade
2 tablespoons balsamic vinegar
1/2 teaspoon Creole mustard
1/2 teaspoon salt
1 teaspoon McCormick Coarse Ground Black Pepper
1/2 cup olive oil

Prepare the meat marinade. In a medium bowl, add the vinegar, Worcestershire, garlic, mustard, salt, pepper, and thyme. Whisk together. Continue whisking while slowly pouring in the olive oil. Place the meat in a large sealable bag and pour the marinade on top. Refrigerate overnight.

Chop the peppers and onion into pieces the same size as the steak cubes. Place in a sealable plastic bag. Add the potatoes to the same plastic bag. In a small bowl, prepare the vegetable marinade. Whisk together the vinegar, mustard, salt, and pepper while slowly adding the olive oil. Pour the marinade over the vegetables. Seal and store in the refrigerator overnight.

Transfer the refrigerated containers in a cooler to your tailgate.

Either the morning before the tailgate or on-site, prepare the kabobs. Soak wooden skewers in water to cover for half an hour before assembling the kabobs. Alternate pieces of meat, vegetables, and potatoes on the skewers. Grill over medium heat until the steak has cooked. Serve on a platter for guests to pick up and eat.

Chicken–Sweet Potato Kabobs

If your tailgate guests aren't the steak and potato crowd, try these tasty Chicken–Sweet Potato Kabobs. By making all the peppers orange, Texas fans who don't want to eat their mascot on game day can make a "burnt" orange kabob for their tailgate.

MAKES 12 KABOBS

2 pounds boneless, skinless chicken breasts, cut into bite-sized cubes
1 red bell pepper
1 yellow bell pepper
1 orange bell pepper
1 medium yellow onion
2 pounds sweet potatoes, peeled, cut into bite-sized pieces, and
    parboiled until fork tender

Chicken Marinade

1/3 cup white balsamic vinegar

2 tablespoons Lea & Perrins Marinade for Chicken

2 teaspoons Dijon mustard

1 teaspoon salt

1/2 teaspoon McCormick Coarse Ground Black Pepper

1/2 teaspoon ground sage

1/2 cup olive oil

Vegetable Marinade

2 tablespoons white balsamic vinegar

1/2 teaspoon salt

1/2 teaspoon Dijon mustard

1/2 teaspoon McCormick Coarse Ground Black Pepper

1/2 cup olive oil

Prepare the chicken marinade. In a medium-sized bowl, combine the vinegar, Lea & Perrins Marinade, mustard, salt, pepper, and sage. Whisk together. Continue whisking while slowly pouring in the olive oil. Add the chicken to a large sealable bag and pour the marinade over them. Seal and refrigerate overnight.

Chop the peppers and onion into bite-sized pieces the same size as the chicken. Add to a plastic sealable bag, along with the sweet potatoes. In a separate medium-sized bowl, prepare the vegetable marinade. Add the vinegar, salt, mustard, and pepper. Whisk together. Continue whisking while slowly drizzling in the olive oil. Pour the vegetable marinade over the vegetables. Seal and store in the refrigerator overnight.

Transfer the refrigerated containers in a cooler to your tailgate.

Assemble the kabobs at home or on-site. Soak wooden skewers in water to cover for half an hour before assembling the kabobs. Alternate pieces of chicken, vegetables, and sweet potatoes on the skewers. Grill on a medium-high grill for 12–15 minutes, until the vegetables are softened and the chicken is cooked. Remove from the grill and serve.

Lemon-Scallion Rice

For a kabob bowl, remove cooked kabobs from the skewers and serve them in a bowl over this fragrant and delicious Lemon-Scallion Rice.

MAKES 6 SERVINGS

4 cups chicken stock
3 tablespoons unsalted butter
1 tablespoon grated lemon zest
1 teaspoon salt
$\frac{1}{2}$ teaspoon McCormick Coarse Ground Black Pepper
$\frac{1}{2}$ cup chopped scallions (white and green parts)
2 cups white long-grain rice

The night before the tailgate, add the chicken stock, butter, lemon zest, salt, and pepper to a sealable container and refrigerate overnight. Refrigerate the scallions in a small sealable container. Measure out the rice and store in a sealable container. Transport the refrigerated containers in a cooler to your tailgate.

At your tailgate, pour the stock mixture into a large heavy-bottomed pot and bring to a boil. Add the rice. Stir and cover. Reduce heat to low and simmer for 20 minutes. Remove from heat and fold in the scallions. Cover the top of the pot with a clean dishtowel for 10 minutes. Serve in bowls and top with kabobs.

Sally's Boneless Barbecue Chicken

Sally's Boneless Barbecue Chicken has been the cornerstone of many family meals. It can be served as a sandwich with bacon, cheddar cheese, and onion rings (page 85) or on a plate with Roasted Sweet Potato Salad (page 92) and hushpuppies (page 114). The tangy vinegar-based marinade is incredibly versatile and makes this a dish you'll never tire of.

MAKES 6–8 SERVINGS

6 boneless, skinless chicken breasts (3–3 ½ pounds)

Marinade

3 tablespoons apple cider vinegar

7 teaspoons light brown sugar

2 tablespoons tomato paste

2 tablespoons lemon juice

1 tablespoon chopped garlic

2 teaspoons crushed red pepper flakes

1 teaspoon Tabasco sauce

1 teaspoon salt

¼ teaspoon McCormick Coarse Ground Black Pepper

½ cup corn oil

In a medium-sized bowl, mix together the vinegar, brown sugar, tomato paste, lemon juice, chopped garlic, red pepper flakes, Tabasco, salt, and pepper. While whisking, slowly pour in the oil. Place the chicken breasts in a large sealable bag. Pour the marinade over the chicken breasts. Seal and refrigerate overnight. Transport to the tailgate in a cooler.

At the tailgate, cook the chicken breasts on a grill until an internal temperature of 165° is reached. Remove them from the grill and let them rest for 5 minutes before serving.

Grilled Baby-Back Ribs

Grilled Baby-Back Ribs

These ribs can be cooked in around 1½ hours, so they are perfect for tailgaters who have a limited time on campus before the game. They are wonderful with just the dry rib rub or sauced with your favorite barbecue sauce.

MAKES 4 SERVINGS

2 (1½-pound) racks of baby-back pork ribs

Rub
2 tablespoons paprika
1½ teaspoons salt
½ teaspoon black pepper
½ teaspoon sugar
¼ teaspoon ground cumin
Pinch of ground cloves

The night before the tailgate, prepare the ribs. Use a knife to trim away any excess quantities of fat. Remove the white membrane from the ribs' underside by piercing the membrane with a small knife and running a finger between the membrane and the ribs. Hold the ribs with one hand while pulling off the membrane with the other. Wrap the ribs tightly in plastic wrap and refrigerate overnight. In a sealable bag or container, add the paprika, salt, pepper, sugar, cumin, and cloves. Seal and shake until blended. Adding the rub to the ribs prior to arriving at the tailgate could cause them to dry out, so wait until you're on-site.

On the morning of the game, pack the ribs in a cooler for transport. Keep them in the cooler until you're ready to cook them. When you're ready to grill, remove the plastic wrap and lay the ribs on a clean surface. Examine the ribs. If one end is drastically thinner than the other or the grill isn't wide enough, cut the rack in half.

Shake the spice container. Rub each rack with the rub mixture, covering all surfaces.

Wrap each section of ribs tightly in aluminum foil. Flip the rack over and wrap in a second tight layer of aluminum foil. Place on a medium grill (325–375°). Close the grill and let the ribs cook for 30 minutes, then flip them over and cook under a closed grill for an additional 30 minutes. Remove from the grill and let them rest for 10 minutes.

Remove the ribs from the foil and serve. Or, if you like your ribs wet, place the ribs back on the grill without the aluminum foil and baste with your favorite barbecue sauce. Grill over low heat for a few minutes until the sauce has formed a thick, sticky glaze.

Chicken Quarters with Taylor's Barbecue Sauce

My favorite cut of chicken to grill is the leg quarter section. With the thigh connected to the leg, your guests can grab one with a piece of waxed paper and eat where they're standing. Since this recipe calls for bone-in chicken, set up the charcoal grill for indirect heat. Line up the coals on one side of the grill to create two zones. The direct zone, which is above the coals, is used for crisping the chicken. The indirect zone, with no coals below, is for cooking the chicken. My favorite way to sauce leg quarters is with Taylor's Barbecue Sauce.

MAKES 4 SERVINGS

4 chicken leg quarters, seasoned with salt and pepper if desired

Taylor's Barbecue Sauce (makes about 2 1/2 cups)
4 tablespoons unsalted butter
1 cup finely chopped onions
2 teaspoons minced garlic
1 1/2 teaspoons paprika
1/2 teaspoon red pepper flakes
1 cup ketchup
1/2 cup light brown sugar
1/3 cup apple cider vinegar
1/4 cup unsulphured molasses (like Grandma's Original)
4 teaspoons lemon juice
1/2 teaspoon dry mustard
1/4 teaspoon salt
1/4 teaspoon pepper

The night before the tailgate, make the barbecue sauce. In a medium pot, melt the butter over medium heat. Add the onions and garlic. Cook on low heat for 10 minutes, stirring occasionally until the onions are soft and translucent. Add the paprika and red pepper flakes and stir. Add the rest of the ingredients and stir. Cook at a low simmer, uncovered, for 1 hour, stirring frequently. Don't let the sauce boil. Remove from heat and cool. Store in a sealable container and refrigerate overnight. Pack the chicken in a sealable container and refrigerate overnight. Transport the refrigerated containers to your tailgate in a cooler.

At your tailgate, set up a charcoal grill with indirect heat. Grease the grill grates. Once the grill is hot, lay the chicken pieces, skin-side up, on the side of the grill with no coals underneath. Place the thigh closer to the coals. Cover and cook until the internal temperature of the chicken is 165°, which will take around 40 minutes. About 10 minutes before the chicken is done, liberally brush the barbecue sauce on the skin side of the chicken. Once it's done, transfer the chicken to the part of the grill with the coals. Place the pieces skin-side down and cook for a few minutes to crisp the skin. Flip them over and baste with more sauce. Remove the pieces from the grill and let them rest for a few minutes before serving.

Teriyaki Pork Tenderloin

One of my most memorable tailgating experiences was aboard Keith Casey's boat in Knoxville, Tennessee. After boating to the game, we tied up next to other tailgaters in the Vol Navy, and Keith grilled up a delicious teriyaki pork tenderloin on the back of his boat. The memories of tailgating on the water, looking out at Neyland Stadium, and eating a delicious pork tenderloin are ones I'll never forget. This tenderloin is inspired by that meal.

MAKES 8 SERVINGS

3 pounds pork tenderloin, trimmed

Marinade
⅓ cup fresh ginger, peeled and chopped into small pieces
⅓ cup soy sauce
¼ cup chopped shallots
3 tablespoons honey
3 tablespoons sesame oil
1 tablespoon finely chopped garlic
½ teaspoon McCormick Coarse Ground Black Pepper
¼ teaspoon crushed red pepper flakes
¼ teaspoon Tabasco sauce
⅓ cup canola oil

In a medium-sized bowl, whisk together the ginger, soy sauce, shallots, honey, sesame oil, garlic, pepper, red pepper flakes, and Tabasco. While whisking, pour in the canola oil. Place the tenderloin in a large sealable plastic bag. Pour the marinade into the bag to cover the tenderloin. Seal the bag and refrigerate overnight. Transport to your tailgate in a cooler.

When ready to grill, place the tenderloin on an oiled grill and cook until an internal temperature of 145° is reached. Remove from the grill, lightly cover with foil, and let rest for 10 minutes. Remove the foil and serve.

Teriyaki Pork
Tenderloin

Garlic-Rosemary Pork Tenderloin

The full-bodied flavors of garlic and rosemary really come through in this pork dish. Garlic-Rosemary Pork Tenderloin shines when sliced in medallions and served with New Potato Salad (page 90) and Carrot-Raisin Salad (page 94). It's equally delicious on a sandwich roll with Jalapeño Hummus (page 63) and Confetti Slaw (page 112).

MAKES 8 SERVINGS

3 pounds pork tenderloin, trimmed

Marinade
$\frac{2}{3}$ cup good-quality red wine
$\frac{1}{3}$ cup balsamic vinegar
$\frac{1}{4}$ cup chopped shallots
3 tablespoons finely chopped garlic
2 tablespoons Worcestershire sauce
1 tablespoon finely chopped rosemary leaves
1 teaspoon Tabasco sauce
1 teaspoon salt
$\frac{1}{2}$ teaspoon McCormick Coarse Ground Black Pepper
$\frac{1}{3}$ cup olive oil

In a medium-sized bowl, whisk together the wine, vinegar, shallots, garlic, Worcestershire, rosemary, Tabasco, salt, and pepper. While whisking, pour in the olive oil. Place the tenderloin in a large sealable plastic bag. Pour the marinade into the bag, covering the tenderloin. Seal the bag and refrigerate overnight. Transport to your tailgate in a cooler.

Grill the tenderloin until it reaches an internal temperature of 145°. Remove from the grill, lightly cover in foil, and let rest 10 minutes before serving. Remove the foil and serve.

Southern Rivalries

In the South, rivalry is much more than a seven-letter word. Rivalries cause entire fan bases to not ever utter certain words, wear certain colors, or spend money in certain cities. Rivalries can tear families apart and even prevent marriages. There's no rational explanation for why some fan bases go to these extremes. Rivalries in college football aren't rational. They are the products of decades and continue to grow stronger with each passing season.

Every school has a rival. Some schools have more than one. You may lose the rest of the season, but when your rival comes to town, it's a must-win game.

The tailgating areas surrounding a stadium have a different intensity when a rival comes to town. Rivalry games spur the largest, longest, and most anticipated tailgates of the season. There are two types of rivalry games: in-state and neighboring-state.

In-State Rivalries

In-state rivalries are among the oldest in football and are played every year, regardless of which conference each school happens to be in. In these games, teams are playing for more than just a win or a loss. They are playing to find out who is the best team in the state. The winner will take home a game trophy, while the loser will have the entire off-season to think about the loss. These games and tailgates draw the largest and most intense crowds of the season.

Here are some of the South's oldest in-state rivalries, matchups that, over the last century, have earned nicknames among their fan bases:

- ▶ "Clean, Old-Fashioned Hate" (Georgia v. Georgia Tech)

- ▶ "The Iron Bowl" (Auburn v. Alabama)
- ▶ "The Palmetto Bowl" (Clemson v. South Carolina)
- ▶ "The Commonwealth Cup" (Virginia v. Virginia Tech)
- ▶ "The Egg Bowl" (Ole Miss v. Mississippi State)
- ▶ "The Bedlam Series" (Oklahoma v. Oklahoma State)
- ▶ "The Oldest Small College Rivalry in the South" (Randolph-Macon v. Hampden-Sydney College)

Neighboring-State Rivalries

Rivalries between interstate schools are an exciting way to end the football season. There are dozens of midseason rivalries that make for great tailgates. When schools in neighboring states face off, there's a border war with conference standing on the line. Here are some of the oldest and most heated border wars in the South, matchups that, over the last century, have also earned nicknames among fans:

- ▶ "Third Saturday in October" (Tennessee v. Alabama)
- ▶ "The South's Oldest Rivalry" (Virginia v. North Carolina)
- ▶ "The Deep South's Oldest Rivalry" (Auburn v. Georgia)
- ▶ "The Red River Rivalry" (Oklahoma v. Texas)
- ▶ "The Magnolia Bowl" (Ole Miss v. LSU)

For rivalry games, more is on the line than just a win or a loss. If your team wins, you have bragging rights for the rest of the year. Reminders of these rivalries extend beyond the tailgate. If you're an Auburn Tigers fan and the Tigers beat Alabama to win the Iron Bowl, you take pride in flying your blue and orange flag for the rest of the year to remind your Alabama alumnus neighbor every day of that loss. University of Georgia fans working in Atlanta are bound to come across Georgia Tech fans in the workplace. It should come as no surprise that friendly workplace bets are often the result.

Football rivalries are even common within families. When spouses are alumni of rival schools, it's known as a "house divided." I grew up in a house divided. My mom is a Duke alumna, and my dad went to the University of North Carolina. When these two schools faced off, there was always one parent who wasn't happy after the game. In Columbia at a tailgate for the South Carolina–Clemson game, I witnessed how these rivalries can divide parent and child. In the fairground lots out-

side Williams-Brice Stadium, I came across a tailgating setup that was orange and purple as well as black and garnet. The SUV was adorned with Clemson paraphernalia, while the tablecloth and tent were clearly showing support for USC. As it turned out, this tailgating family was divided. The parents were both Clemson alums, but the oldest daughter was a junior at USC. A compromise had to happen. The deal was that the daughter would secure the parking spot on the condition that her father would limit the amount of orange he brought. While the members of this family love one another and on a normal Saturday would get along perfectly, this day was not normal. This was Palmetto Bowl game day. Bragging rights were on the line, and one side of the family wasn't going home happy. ■

A divided grill at the Clemson versus South Carolina game in Columbia

Grilled Oysters

Grilled Oysters

Grilled oysters are a common sight on southern campuses near the Atlantic and Gulf coasts. Each oyster cooks at its own rate, so gather around the grill and socialize with your friends as the oysters cook. Everyone can pick out the ones they'll eat and watch patiently for them to open. Once an oyster is open, scoop it up before someone else does.

MAKES 8–12 SERVINGS

2 dozen oysters

Purchase the oysters the day before or the morning of the tailgate. If you're holding them overnight, keep them refrigerated.

At the tailgate, check through the oysters and discard any that have already opened. Make sure you cook only the oysters that are completely sealed. Place the oysters on a medium-high grill. Every oyster is a slightly different size, so cooking times will vary. Leave them on the grill until you can see the shells open. Once opened, remove the oysters from the grill with an insulated glove or cooking towel. Using an oyster shucker, open the shells and let your guests remove the cooked meat from inside. Discard the shells. While it may not be necessary for purists, your guests will appreciate the offer of saltine crackers, lemon wedges, and hot sauce or cocktail sauce.

Clifton's Tenders with Peach-Bourbon
Dipping Sauce

Clifton's Tenders with Peach-Bourbon Dipping Sauce

My brother Clifton's favorite food is chicken tenders. Even on Thanksgiving, he eats tenders, not turkey. I see boxes, buckets, and platters of catered or fast-food chicken all the time at tailgates. These are delicious, but why would you order a tray of chicken that was cooked hours ago when you can impress your guests by frying up fresh batches of tenders on-site? A camp oven will keep the tenders warm while you fry them in batches.

MAKES 4 SERVINGS

Peach-Bourbon Dipping Sauce
1 (15 ¼-ounce) can of peaches in heavy syrup
3 tablespoons dark brown sugar
3 tablespoons bourbon
3 tablespoons diced dry apricots
2 tablespoons unsalted butter
2 tablespoons lemon juice
½ teaspoon salt
¼ teaspoon Tabasco sauce

Chicken Tenders
1½ pounds chicken tenderloins (tenders)
2 cups buttermilk
Peanut oil for frying

Dredge
5 cups self-rising flour
1 tablespoon salt
2 teaspoons McCormick Coarse Ground Black Pepper

Wash
1½ cups 2 percent milk
1 large egg

The night before the tailgate, make the Peach-Bourbon Dipping Sauce. Put all the sauce ingredients into a saucepan. Stir over medium heat until the butter melts. Raise the temperature to medium-high while stirring and bring to a boil. Reduce to a simmer and let simmer for 15 minutes, stirring occasionally. Remove from heat and let cool for 15 minutes. Purée the sauce in a food processor or blender. Store in a sealable container and refrigerate overnight.

Place the chicken tenders and buttermilk in a sealable container and refrigerate overnight. Mix the dredge ingredients in a sealable container. Mix the milk and egg in a sealable container and refrigerate overnight. The morning of the tailgate, remove the chicken from the buttermilk and pack in a sealable container. Transport the refrigerated containers in a cooler to your tailgate.

At your tailgate, coat the tenders completely in the dredge. Dip them in the wash and then back in the dredge. Fry at 360° until cooked through, about 4–4½ minutes. Drain on brown paper bags and store in a 275° camp oven until served. Serve with Peach-Bourbon Dipping Sauce or blue cheese dressing (page 178).

Fried Frog Legs

If you and your guests are looking for something that will put a little bit of a hop in your step, try some frog legs. Eaten like chicken wings, they are a unique item to have at your tailgate. If your team is playing Texas Christian University's Horned Frogs, this dish is the perfect way to show your opinion of the opponent.

MAKES 6–8 SERVINGS

3 pounds (4–6 count) frog legs
Peanut oil for frying

Brine
1 cup boiling water
2 tablespoons kosher salt
2 tablespoons dark brown sugar
4 teaspoons chopped garlic
1 tablespoon lemon juice
$\frac{1}{4}$ teaspoon whole black peppercorns
4 cups cold water
2 lemons, sliced thin
1 yellow onion, sliced thin

Dredge
4 cups self-rising flour
1 cup self-rising yellow cornmeal
1 tablespoon salt
2 teaspoons McCormick Coarse Ground Black Pepper
$\frac{1}{2}$ teaspoon garlic powder

Wash
3 cups 2 percent milk
2 eggs

Fried Frog Legs

If the frog legs are frozen, let them thaw completely, then place them in a large sealable container. In a large bowl, pour the boiling water over the salt and brown sugar. Stir until the salt and sugar have dissolved. Add the garlic, lemon juice, peppercorns, and cold water and stir. Add the lemon slices, onion slices, and frog legs and refrigerate for 3 hours. Remove the frog legs from the brine and rinse them in cold water. Pack in a sealable container and refrigerate overnight. Mix the dredge ingredients in a sealable container. Mix the wash of milk and eggs in a sealable container and refrigerate overnight. Transport the refrigerated containers in a cooler to your tailgate.

When you're ready to fry the frog legs, roll them in the dredge, completely coating them in an even layer of dredge. Dip them in the wash and then back in the dredge. Shake off any excess dredge and fry for about 7 minutes in 370° oil. Once they are golden brown and cooked through, remove them from the oil and let them drain on a sheet pan lined with brown paper bags or paper towels.

Fried Alligator Strips

If you've never had alligator before, tailgaters in Baton Rouge will fix that. At LSU, I was exposed to a Cajun fry basket filled with gator, shrimp, and frog legs. Playing the Florida Gators? This is the perfect food to "eat the competition" with. If you don't live in an area of the country that offers fresh alligator, you can order it online and have it overnighted to your door.

SERVES 4–6

2 pounds alligator meat, cut into strips or bite-sized cubes
Peanut oil for frying

Buttermilk Marinade
4 cups buttermilk
½ teaspoon salt
½ teaspoon crushed red pepper flakes
½ teaspoon McCormick Coarse Ground Black Pepper

Dredge

4 cups self-rising flour

1 cup self-rising yellow cornmeal

1 tablespoon salt

2 teaspoons McCormick Coarse Ground Black Pepper

½ teaspoon cayenne pepper

Wash

1½ cups 2 percent milk

1 egg

If the meat is frozen, completely thaw it before cutting it into bite-sized pieces. Place the cut pieces into a large sealable container. Mix the buttermilk, salt, red pepper flakes, and pepper and pour it over the alligator meat. Store in the refrigerator overnight. Mix together the dredge ingredients and store in a sealable container. Mix together the milk and egg in a shallow sealable container and refrigerate overnight. The morning of your tailgate, drain the excess marinade from the meat. Pack the alligator meat in a sealable bag. Transport the refrigerated containers in a cooler to your tailgate.

When ready to fry the gator, remove the meat from the bag and evenly coat each piece with the dredge. Dip it in the wash and then back in the dredge. Shake off any excess dredge. Fry at around 370° until the meat is golden brown and cooked through, about 3 minutes. Remove from the fryer and drain on a sheet pan lined with paper bags or paper towels.

Shrimp boil prepared by fans of East Carolina in Greenville, North Carolina

Shrimp Boil

I saw shrimp boils from Auburn to East Carolina. They're easy to prepare and feed a whole lot of people at once, and their communal serving style is perfect for simultaneous socializing and eating. This dish should be cooked over a single propane burner in a large pot, like a 30-quart aluminum pot, fitted with a strainer basket. The basket will allow for the contents of the boil to be removed safely and easily.

MAKES 8–10 SERVINGS

3 gallons water

1 cup crab boil seasoning

5 lemons, halved

4 teaspoons kosher salt

2 large bay leaves

3 jalapeños, ends removed

2 tablespoons whole peppercorns

5 garlic cloves, peeled and smashed

3 pounds new potatoes

4–5 large carrots, cut into thirds

2 medium yellow onions, halved

2 medium red onions, halved

2 pounds smoked sausage, cut into 1$\frac{1}{2}$-inch segments

5 ears of corn, cut in half

3 pounds large unpeeled shrimp

Add the water to the pot. Add the crab boil seasoning, squeeze in the lemon juice, and toss in the lemons. Add the salt, bay leaves, jalapeños, peppercorns, and garlic. Bring to a boil. Add the potatoes, stir, and cook for 10 minutes. Add the carrots, stir, and cook for 5 minutes. Add the onions, stir, and cook for 3 minutes. Add the sausage and corn, stir, and cook for about 5 more minutes until the carrots and potatoes are fork tender. Add the shrimp and cook until pink and no longer translucent, around 2–3 minutes. Remove the bay leaves.

Slowly lift the strainer basket and drain the excess water into the pot. Pour the boil into aluminum roasting pans or spread across a plastic-lined table surface. Serve with plenty of melted butter, crusty bread, lemon slices, hot sauce, salt, and pepper.

Eating Your Competition

On game day, don't settle for beating your opponent; "eat" the competition. Take the disdain you feel toward the competition and channel it into a delicious and creative meal that will inspire your fellow fans and intimidate the opposition. Every school has a mascot, so "eating the competition" is something you can do for every game. All you need is a little bit of creativity.

Live Mascots

Certain teams have live versions of their mascots that are important parts of their schools' identities. Almost all of them lead the team in the pregame player walk, stand on the sidelines during games, or make an appearance on campus during game day. If you want to intimidate your opponent, serving mascot-inspired menu items is a great way to do so. Here are a few of the live mascots seen throughout the South and some suggestions of how you can incorporate them into your game-day spread.

TEAM	MASCOT	DISH
University of Arkansas	Tusk the Russian Boar	Grilled Baby-Back Ribs (page 129)
University of North Carolina	Rameses the Ram	Any mutton or lamb dish
University of Texas	Bevo the Longhorn Steer	Steak and Creamer Potato Kabobs (page 123)

Birds

I certainly wouldn't eat an eagle, owl, or ibis on game day, but any type of poultry can make a plausible substitute. This could be Clifton's Tenders (page 139), Chicken Quarters with Taylor's Barbecue Sauce (page 130), Sally's Boneless Barbecue Chicken (page 127), or Smoked Beer-Can Chicken (page 150). Some teams with avian mascots:

TEAM	MASCOT
Auburn University	Nova the Golden Eagle and Spirit the Bald Eagle
Coastal Carolina University	Maddox the Rooster
Florida Atlantic University	Hera the Eurasian Eagle Owl
Georgia Southern University	Freedom the Bald Eagle
University of South Carolina	Sir Big Spur the Gamecock

Horses

Horses are an important part of many teams' game-day traditions. When playing these schools, hamburgers can be renamed "horseburgers," and during colder games, you could call the beef in your Chow-Down Chili (page 160) "horse meat." Here are some teams that have horses as mascots:

TEAM	MASCOT
Florida State University	Renegade the Appaloosa
Murray State University	Racer One the Thoroughbred
Oklahoma State University	Bullet the Quarter Horse
Southern Methodist University	Peruna the Shetland Pony
Texas Tech University	Midnight Matador the Quarter Horse
University of Central Florida	Pegasus the Lipizzan Stallion
University of Virgina	Sabre
University of Oklahoma	Boomer and Sooner

Dogs

You would also never actually eat a dog at your tailgate, but on game day, you might try claiming that the hot dogs and sausages are "hot dawgs" made out of, say, bulldog. Sandwich Chili (page 180) could have imagined bits of collie, Tamaskan, or hound in it. Dog mascots in the South include these:

TEAM	MASCOT
Louisiana Tech University	Tech the Bulldog
Mississippi State University	Bully the Bulldog
North Carolina State University	Tuffy the Tamaskan
Texas A&M University	Reveille the Collie
University of Georgia	UGA the Bulldog
University of Tennessee	Smokey the Bluetick Coonhound

Louisiana State fans transforming a pig into an "elephant" to eat the competition for the LSU versus Alabama game

Tigers and Bears

You wouldn't likely eat tiger or bear, either, but on game day, a huge pork tenderloin becomes a tiger loin, chicken nuggets are tiger toes, and Red Sangria (page 20) or a Razzle Dazzle Cocktail (page 17) is tiger's blood. Brunswick Stew (page 173) becomes bear meat stew.

TEAM	MASCOT
Baylor University	Joy and Lady the Black Bears
Louisiana State University	Mike the Tiger
University of Memphis	Tom the Tiger

If your rival isn't on one of these lists, don't worry. Not all schools bring live mascots to games. In Gainesville, you won't see a live alligator on the sidelines. At Texas Christian University, you won't find a live horned frog leading the team into the stadium. You can, however, still serve Fried Alligator Strips (page 142) or Fried Frog Legs (page 141) at your tailgate. If you're playing Maryland, you don't have to eat terrapin, but why not serve chocolate turtles for dessert?

For mascots that aren't animals, it just takes a little more creativity. Playing against Duke? Deviled eggs or devil's food cake are perfect ways to serve Blue Devil on your game-day menu.

When I tailgated at LSU, I saw a group of Tiger fans who showed great creativity in creating a menu around Alabama's mascot, an elephant. These fans cooked two whole pigs. While one of the pigs looked normal, the second had been transformed. Extra skin was added to create large elephant ears and a trunk. By using their imaginations and thinking creatively, these Tiger fans found a very visible way to eat an "elephant" on game day.

The only limit to your menu is your imagination and creativity. Many tailgaters have found that "eating the competition" isn't just for the big games and that every opponent's mascot inspires their game-day menus. If you don't already plan your menu around a theme, I suggest you give "eating the competition" a try. It's a great way to show your game-day spirit and have a delicious meal at the same time. ■

Dry-Brined Turkey Breast

Dry brining is a great way to add another layer of flavor to your smoked turkey. Unlike the more familiar wet-brining process, dry brining doesn't require any liquid or large containers. This turkey is delicious on a sandwich, eaten plain, or in Smoked Turkey Salad (page 105).

MAKES 8 SERVINGS

1 (6–6½ pound) turkey breast (if frozen, thaw completely)

Dry-Brine Seasoning
4 teaspoons kosher salt
1 teaspoon grated lemon zest
1 tablespoon grated orange zest
1¼ teaspoons rubbed sage
¾ teaspoon sugar

In a small bowl, mix together the salt, lemon zest, orange zest, sage, and sugar. Rinse the turkey breast and pat dry. Liberally rub the surface and under the skin with the seasoning mixture. Refrigerate the turkey breast uncovered, breast-side up, on a rack placed over a plate or baking sheet. On game day, place the turkey in a sealable plastic bag or container and transport in a cooler to your tailgate.

At your tailgate, prepare the smoker with a 1 to 2 ratio of soaked applewood chips to hickory chips, according to the manufacturer's instructions. Smoke at around 240° until the internal temperature of the breast is 165°. When checking the breast's internal temperature, check in the thickest part, avoiding the bone. Plan for at least 45–50 minutes per pound, but it may take more or less time, depending on the weather conditions and your smoking equipment.

Once an internal temperature of 165° has been reached, remove the breast from the smoker, cover it in foil, and let it rest for 30 minutes before carving.

Smoked Beer-Can Chicken

Smoked Beer-Can Chicken is the moistest chicken you'll ever eat. Use whatever beer you're drinking at your tailgate. I suggest you invest in a beer-can chicken stand. You can find one in the hardware or grilling section of a home goods store or online. Once the chicken is cooked, I like to pull off a piece of meat and eat it on soft white bread with a dollop of Taylor's Barbecue Sauce (page 130).

MAKES 4 SERVINGS

1 (5-pound) fresh fryer chicken
1 teaspoon salt
1 teaspoon garlic powder
1 teaspoon black pepper
1 teaspoon grated lemon zest
1 can of beer
1 smashed garlic clove

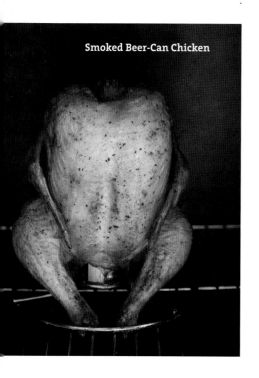

Smoked Beer-Can Chicken

The night before the tailgate, remove the chicken from its packaging and rinse. Remove the neck, giblets, and anything else from inside the chicken's body cavity. Pat it dry with paper towels. Wrap it in plastic wrap and refrigerate it in a sealable container. On game day, pack the chicken in a cooler. Mix together the salt, garlic powder, pepper, and lemon zest and pack in a sealable container.

On-site, prepare the smoker with hickory chips according to the manufacturer's instructions. Open the can of beer and pour about half of it into a plastic cup to drink while the chicken is smoking. Add the smashed garlic clove to the beer can. On a clean sheet pan, place the beer can into the beer-can chicken holder. Place the chicken upright on top of the beer can, inserting the beer can into the cavity. Rub the outside of the chicken with the salt, garlic powder, pepper, and lemon zest mixture. Cook at around 240° for 3–3½ hours. The chicken is done when the center of the breast meat reaches 165°.

Once the breast meat reaches the correct temperature, remove the chicken from the smoker and let it rest for 10 minutes on a sheet pan. Remove the chicken from the beer can and allow guests to choose their favorite parts.

Applewood-Smoked Turkey Legs

There's something fun about holding a giant smoked turkey leg in one hand and a can of beer in the other. Their large size and portable nature make turkey legs the perfect food for the tailgater on the move. With turkey leg in one hand and beverage in the other, you'll never go hungry as you make your way around campus.

MAKES 6 SERVINGS

8 cups boiling water
¼ cup salt
¼ cup dark brown sugar
½ teaspoon crushed red pepper flakes
8 cups cold water
6 turkey legs
Salt and pepper
Taylor's Barbecue Sauce (page 130) for basting

The night before the game, brine the turkey legs. Add the boiling water to a large container. Add the salt, brown sugar, and red pepper flakes. Stir until the salt and sugar have dissolved. Add the cold water and let the brine cool. Add the turkey legs, covering with the brine. Cover and refrigerate overnight.

The morning of the game, remove the legs from the brine and rinse under cold water. Pat dry with paper towels and season with salt and pepper. Store in a sealable container and refrigerate. Pack in a cooler to transport to your tailgate.

On-site, prepare the smoker with a 2 to 1 ratio of soaked apple-wood chips to hickory chips. Smoke the turkey legs at around 240° for about 3 hours. During the last half hour of cooking, baste with Taylor's Barbecue Sauce. Continue smoking until the turkey legs reach an internal temperature of 165°. Let the legs rest for 10 minutes before serving. Serve with wax paper so guests can hold the turkey legs in their hands.

Applewood-Smoked
Turkey Legs

Smoked Pork Shoulder

Smoked Pork Shoulder

It would be hard to find anyone who would turn down a pulled-pork sandwich, especially one you smoked and pulled at your tailgate. Pork shoulders are perfect for the all-day tailgater. They fit in a standard-sized backyard smoker and will cook all day as you enjoy socializing with your guests.

MAKES 8 SERVINGS

1 (6–6½ pound) bone-in pork shoulder
½ cup paprika
2 tablespoons pepper
3 tablespoons kosher salt
2 teaspoons sugar

The night before the tailgate, remove the shoulder from its packaging and rinse. With a sharp knife, trim off any large areas of exterior fat from the top and the sides. You may trim off some of the fat from the large fat cap on the bottom, but don't remove it all. It will help insulate the meat while it cooks. After the meat is trimmed, pat it dry with paper towels.

In a small bowl, mix together the rub of paprika, pepper, salt, and sugar. Liberally apply the rub to all areas of the shoulder. Once you think you've applied enough, apply a little more. Tightly wrap the rubbed shoulder in plastic wrap and store in the refrigerator overnight. On game day, transfer the shoulder to a sealable container and place in a cooler. Keep in the cooler until you're ready to cook.

At your tailgate, prepare the smoker according to the manufacturer's instructions. I like using soaked hickory chips. Unwrap the shoulder, place it in the smoker fat-side down, and smoke it at around 240°. Cook the shoulder until the internal temperature reaches 180°. This will take around 1½ hours per pound. A 6-pound butt will take around 9 hours; a 6½-pound butt will take close to 10. If you prefer to smoke the shoulder at a lower temperature, it will take even longer. The smoker may vary in heat throughout this process, weather elements may effect cooking, and every shoulder is a little different, so keep give yourself plenty of time if you're planning to smoke a shoulder.

Once the shoulder has reached 180°, remove it from the smoker and wrap it in aluminum foil. If you won't be eating for a few hours yet, you can place the shoulder in a dry cooler (no ice) surrounded with dry towels to keep it warm for a few hours. I've seen some tailgaters use the cooler method for noon games. They cook the shoulder overnight, and on the morning of the game, they transport it in a towel-filled cooler.

After the shoulder has rested for at least 30 minutes, remove it from the aluminum foil. Wearing gloves, tear apart the shoulder meat, discarding any large pieces of fat. Place the torn pork in an aluminum roasting pan and cover with foil. Allow your guests to assemble their own sandwiches. Serve with Hog Wash (recipe follows).

Hog Wash

This simple vinegar sauce is what I like to put on my pulled-pork sandwich. A few splashes is all you need to enhance an already delicious meal. Make it 2–3 days before the tailgate and store in the refrigerator until game day.

MAKES ABOUT 2½ CUPS

1 cup white vinegar
1 cup apple cider vinegar
⅓ cup ketchup
2 teaspoons salt
1 teaspoon red pepper flakes
1 teaspoon black pepper

Add all the ingredients to a sealable jar and shake until mixed together. Refrigerate until use and transport to your tailgate in a plastic squeeze bottle. Shake before using.

Fish and Grits

On a cold December morning, I came across an Alabama A&M fan with a big cast-iron cauldron and a large pot. Out of the cauldron he pulled a boneless fillet of flaky white fish fried to a crispy golden brown. As the fillet cooled on a layer of paper towels, he scooped a heaping, steaming-hot portion of creamy white grits out of the pot and into a bowl. This bowl of fish and grits was just what I needed to stay warm before kickoff.

MAKES 8 SERVINGS

2 pounds white fish fillets
3 cups buttermilk
Peanut oil for frying

Dredge
4 cups self-rising white cornmeal
2 teaspoons salt
$\frac{1}{2}$ teaspoon McCormick Coarse Ground Black Pepper
$\frac{1}{8}$ teaspoon cayenne pepper

Grits
4 cups whole milk
4 cups water
1 teaspoon salt
3 tablespoons unsalted butter
2 cups white grits
$\frac{1}{4}$ teaspoon McCormick Coarse Ground Black Pepper
Salt to taste

The night before the tailgate, place the buttermilk in a sealable container and refrigerate overnight. Measure out the cornmeal, 2 teaspoons salt, $\frac{1}{2}$ teaspoon black pepper, and cayenne pepper and place in a sealable container. Place the whole milk, water, and 1 teaspoon salt in a sealable container and refrigerate overnight. Pack the butter in a sealable container and refrigerate. Measure out the grits and place in a sealable plastic bag. Transport the refrigerated containers in a cooler to your tailgate.

At the tailgate, cook the fish and grits on a propane burner or stove. If you have two burners, then you can have one person make the grits while another fries the fish. If you have only one burner, make the grits followed by the fish.

To make the grits, pour the milk and water mixture in a large heavy-bottomed pot. Bring to a simmer and add the grits. Turn heat to very low, stir, and cover. Cook, covered, for 15–20 minutes, uncovering to quickly stir the grits every few minutes, until they have reached a smooth consistency. Keep an eye on the grits; the depth of the pot will affect the cooking time, so they may take more or less time to cook than specified. Once the grits have the consistency you desire, stir in the butter, pepper, and salt to taste until the butter is melted and mixed through. Cover and set aside.

An hour before you'll be frying the fish, soak it in the buttermilk. When you're ready to fry the fish, remove it from the buttermilk and place it in the dredge. Completely coat the surface of the fish in the dredge. Remove from the dredge and set on a plate before frying. Fry in oil between 365° and 370° until the fish is golden brown. Remove from the fryer and drain on paper towels. To serve, fill a bowl with a heaping serving of grits and top with the fried fish.

Fish and Grits

The Band's Role in Tailgating

Many tailgaters come to see the players on the field, but there are those who make their way to college football stadiums for the bands. College marching bands put on a well-organized, electrifying, and entertaining show. With names like "Sonic Boom of the South," the "Human Jukebox," and the "Blue & Gold Marching Machine," the bands of college football promise as much excitement as the games on the fields do.

Bands play an important role in creating an enthusiastic game-day atmosphere on college campuses. Their rhythmic beats carry widely as they travel through the tailgating lots before the game. In Gainesville, the "Pride of the Sunshine" band warms up among tailgaters in the Plaza of the Americas. The "Million Dollar Band" gives a pregame concert known as the "Elephant Stomp" on the steps of Gorgas Library in Tuscaloosa. At Georgia games, "The Red Coat Band" performs for thousands as fans wait for the players and coaches to follow the Dawg Walk to the stadium. The largest ROTC band in the world, "The Fightin' Texas Aggie Band," is cheered by thousands when it marches the football team to the stadium on game day in College Station. In Knoxville, the "Pride of the Southland Band" delights the crowd when it creates the iconic T-formation that the players run through.

Every band has one thing in common: its music and sounds are the heartbeat of game days. In Clemson, the band plays the iconic tune of "Tiger Rag." In Chapel Hill, the tune is "I'm a Tarheel Born," while in Fayetteville, it's "Arkansas Fight." Every campus sounds a little different, but the reaction to the band is the same. When the band begins to play, tailgaters all around shake their pom-poms to the tune. Akin to a shot of adrenaline to the heart, the band's rendition of its team's fight song will get any group of tailgaters excited for the game.

At Historically Black Colleges and Universities throughout the South, the competition on the field isn't just for the football team. On game day, the bands compete as well. At fall classics like the Magic City Classic between Alabama A&M and Alabama State, the Bayou Classic between Grambling State and Southern, and the Florida Classic between FAMU and Bethune-Cookman, a battle of the bands takes place.

During the Southwestern Athletic Conference Championship in Birmingham, Alabama, I was able to witness firsthand two amazing bands. Throughout Alabama A&M and Grambling State's hard-tested game on the field, the bands of both schools provided a musical score to the action. When A&M scored, its band would play a tune letting Grambling know. When Grambling made a huge defensive stop on the field, its band was there to respond with a tune of its own. This musical back-and-forth went on throughout the game, but the real show happened during halftime.

At the half, each band had its chance to take the 100-yard stage. I had seen YouTube and TV clips of these bands' performances, but being there—mere yards away—was unlike anything else I had ever seen or heard. The Tiger Marching Band of Grambling State took the field first. It was then followed by the Marching Maroon and White of Alabama A&M. I was mesmerized by the sights and sounds of well over 100 musicians marching and turning on a dime in complete unison. The drum majors led the group with dance moves that, to me, seemed possible only for someone with an elastic spine. All these movements were in step to full and brassy renditions of popular songs from both today and decades past. It was easy to forget I was at a football game while watching showmanship of this quality.

The college band is another aspect of game day that makes tailgating a truly unique event. Bands carry on school traditions and are able to stir up any crowd at will with their fight songs. They are the heartbeat of game day, and it's easy to see why some fans come just to see and hear the band play. ∎

Clockwise from top left: The Alabama A&M band, the Alabama band at the Elephant Stomp in Tuscaloosa, the Fightin' Texas Aggie Band marching toward Kyle Field, and the Florida Gators Color Guard.

Chow-Down Chili

This is a classic thick, meaty, and beany chili. It has assertive but not overbearing heat. This is my family's recipe; it's so good, we eat it year-round. You can make this chili on-site, or if there's an early kickoff, you can make it the night before and reheat it on-site.

MAKES 10–12 SERVINGS

4 tablespoons bacon drippings

4 cups diced yellow onions

2 cups diced green bell peppers

2 jalapeños, seeded and finely chopped

2 tablespoons minced garlic

1 pound bulk Italian sausage

3 pounds ground sirloin

⅓ cup chili powder

⅓ cup ground cumin

1½ teaspoons cayenne pepper

½ teaspoon dried thyme

½ teaspoon ground coriander

1 tablespoon kosher salt

1 teaspoon McCormick Coarse Ground Black Pepper

1 tablespoon Worcestershire sauce

½ teaspoon Tabasco sauce

1 (10-ounce) can of Rotel tomatoes

2 (28-ounce) cans of diced tomatoes

2 (6-ounce) cans of tomato paste

4 cups chicken stock

3 (15-ounce) cans of kidney beans, drained

The night before the tailgate, put the bacon drippings, onions, peppers, and garlic in a sealable container and refrigerate. Put the sausage and the sirloin in a sealable container and refrigerate. Put the chili powder, cumin, cayenne pepper, thyme, coriander, salt, and black pepper in a sealable container. Add the Worcestershire, Tabasco, tomatoes, tomato paste, chicken stock, and kidney beans to a sealable container and refrigerate overnight. Transport the refrigerated containers to your tailgate in a cooler.

In a large pot, add the bacon drippings, onions, peppers, and garlic. Cook over medium heat 5–7 minutes, stirring frequently until the onions are translucent and the peppers are soft. Add the meats. Increase the heat to medium-high and cook, stirring frequently, until the meat is cooked and beginning to brown. Reduce the heat to medium-low. Add the seasonings. Stir frequently and cook for 5 minutes. Add the stock mixture. Cook the chili on a low simmer for 1½ hours, stirring frequently.

The Tailgating Potato

Try ladling a big helping of your favorite chili on top of a warm baked potato. It's filling and will keep you satisfied throughout the game.

MAKES 4 SERVINGS

4 russet potatoes, washed and dried
Olive oil
Kosher salt and black pepper

The morning of the tailgate, rub the skin of the potatoes with enough olive oil to create a thin coating on the outside. Sprinkle each potato with salt and pepper. Tightly wrap the seasoned potatoes in two layers of aluminum foil. Seal off the ends of the foil, making the wrapping airtight. Transport in a cooler to the tailgate.

About an hour before you're ready to eat, place the wrapped potatoes on the grill over low heat. Close the grill's lid and cook the potatoes for about an hour, rotating every 15 minutes. The potatoes are done when a fork easily pierces the skin and penetrates to the center. Spilt the potatoes open and serve with your favorite chili, stew, or other topping.

Chow-Down Chili (p. 160) on top of The Tailgating Potato

Neutral-Site Games

At most college football games, there's a home team and a visiting team. There's an advantage to playing at home. Players are accustomed to the stadium, fans know where to park and tailgate, and the overall atmosphere is one that favors the home team. However, there are exceptions. Certain games of the season are played at neutral sites. In this case, there's no home field advantage, and neither team has a decisive edge. It's up to you, the fan, to be there and to create that home field advantage for your team. Here are three examples of neutral-site games your team could be playing in this season.

Season Kickoff Games

Season opening, neutral-site games affect only a few teams each year. Games are usually played at the Georgia Dome in Atlanta and Cowboys Stadium in Dallas during Labor Day weekend. These kickoff games are a chance for two nationally ranked teams and their fan bases to get together and celebrate the start of a new season. For most fans, the kickoff game has been on the calendar for over a year. They have suffered through an eight-and-a-half-month off-season, thinking and planning for the upcoming season. Each team has a zero in the loss column, and the hope that this will be the year to win it all fills the air.

Midseason Rivalries

Some college football rivalries are so big that playing each other at home doesn't work. They require a neutral site for their yearly meetings. In Dallas, University of Texas and Oklahoma fans converge on the state fairgrounds every October for the Red River Rivalry. Alabama A&M and Alabama State meet annually in the Magic City Classic to settle a rivalry that dates back to the 1920s. Since the mid-1970s, the Bayou Classic between conference rivals Grambling State University and Southern University has taken place at the neutral site of New Orleans.

Every October, the neutral site of Jacksonville, Florida, is completely overtaken by Florida Gator fans and Georgia Bulldog fans. In 2010, I had the pleasure of experiencing this game for myself. Fans from these two schools arrived up to a week in advance to begin their tailgating festivities. Boats from either school docked up at Jacksonville Landing, and RVs rolled into town. With tailgating on both the water and the land around the stadium, the week leading up to the Florida v. Georgia game had the whole city of Jacksonville either in red and black or orange and blue. This rivalry is so intense that many Georgia students refuse to spend the night before the game in the state of Florida. They will instead congregate in St. Simons Island, Georgia, and drive the seventy-five miles to Jacksonville on game day.

Because this is a neutral-site game, all parking lots, neighborhoods, and any places that will accommodate a car are inundated with a mix of Gator and Bulldog fans. With the warm Florida weather and two passionate fan bases, it should come as no surprise that this annual matchup is considered one of the best game-day atmospheres in college football. If you're a Florida or a Georgia fan, this is a game that you hate to miss!

Postseason Tailgating

When the regular season ends, it doesn't mean tailgating is over. Depending on your team's record, you may have an opportunity for postseason tailgating. For postseason play, your options will depend on which division your team belongs in. In the Football Bowl Subdivision (FBS), teams play in conference championship games and bowl games.

The FBS schools' bowl or conference championship games are played at a neutral site. These matchups aren't determined until after the regular season. Tailgaters may have to do some quick planning and make a road trip to cheer their team on. In your planning, make note that many bowl games take place on weeknights and during the end-of-the-year holiday season rather than on the typical Saturday afternoons of the regular season.

If your team isn't a member of the FBS, your postseason is based on a playoff. If you're the higher seed, your playoff game will be at home. These playoff games can allow you up to three additional chances to tailgate at home.

Planning your tailgate menu and theme around the opponent, showing up in large numbers, and tailgating all day are ways you can help shift a neutral site into a home field advantage. Ending your season in a loss makes for a longer-seeming off-season, so showing up and tailgating for your team's postseason matchup is an important way to show support.

In attending a neutral-site game, you're venturing into a stadium that may not have the same rules for tailgating as your home stadium. At home, you may be able to tailgate for twelve hours prior to the game, but at a new stadium, you could be limited to five. This may impact your menu planning; for instance, a pork shoulder can't be smoked on-site in five hours. To avoid catastrophe, always make sure you're up-to-date on the neutral-site stadium's latest tailgating policies before you plan your menu. ■

Florida State fans tailgating before the ACC Championship game in Charlotte, North Carolina

Red Beans and Rice

Large pots filled with red beans and rice are a frequent sight when tailgating in the Bayou. This filling bean dish can be made at the tailgate or prepared the day before, refrigerated, and heated back up on campus. Cook Tailgating Rice, add the beans, and you have a satisfying meal.

MAKES 8–12 SERVINGS

1 (1-pound) bag of dried red kidney beans
2 tablespoons bacon drippings
2 cups chopped yellow onions
1½ cups chopped celery
1 cup chopped green bell peppers
1 cup chopped red bell peppers
2 tablespoons chopped garlic
1–1¼ pounds smoked turkey legs
2 bay leaves
8 cups low- or no-sodium chicken stock
2 teaspoons paprika
½ teaspoon McCormick Coarse Ground Black Pepper
½ teaspoon dried thyme
½ teaspoon dried oregano
½ teaspoon red pepper flakes
½ teaspoon salt
Tailgating Rice (page 165) for serving

The day before the tailgate, rinse the beans. Remove any pebbles and debris. Soak them overnight in a bowl with 2 inches of water above the beans, around 12 hours. The next morning, drain the beans and reserve them until you're ready to cook.

In a large pot over medium heat, add the bacon drippings, onions, celery, peppers, and garlic. Cook, stirring frequently, until the onions are translucent and the peppers soften. Add the beans, turkey legs, bay leaves, and chicken stock and stir. Bring to a boil and stir. Reduce heat to simmer, cover, and cook for 1 hour. Remove the turkey legs and let them cool. Remove the bay leaves. Add the paprika, pepper, thyme, oregano, and red pepper flakes and stir. Simmer uncovered for 30 minutes, stirring occasionally. When the turkey legs have cooled, remove the meat. Chop into bite-sized pieces and add to the red beans.

After the beans have simmered for 30 minutes, use the back of a spoon to press about a fourth of the bean mixture against the side of the pan to thicken the sauce. Add the salt and stir. Reduce to low until served. Serve over the rice.

Tailgating Rice

Rice becomes Tailgating Rice when you cook it on-site. A hot bowl of rice is a versatile dish, ideal for accompanying a thick and rich gumbo or spicy red beans.

MAKES 8–12 SERVINGS

8 cups water
1 teaspoon salt
4 cups long-grain white rice

In a large aluminum pot over a propane burner, add the water and salt. Bring to a boil. Once boiling, add the rice, stir, and turn heat to low. Cover and cook for 20 minutes. Remove from heat and stir. Cover the top of the pot with a clean dishtowel while waiting to serve.

Jambalaya

Jambalaya

I love jambalaya—the way it tastes, the way it smells, the way its name rolls off the tongue. On a cold game day, a hearty bowl of jambalaya hits the spot. By packing the ingredients the night before, you can easily make this dish on-site.

MAKES 10–12 SERVINGS

2 tablespoons bacon drippings

12 boneless, skinless chicken thighs, seasoned with salt and pepper

12–13 ounces andouille sausage, sliced into $\frac{1}{4}$-inch slices

4 cups chopped yellow onions

2$\frac{1}{2}$ cups chopped celery

2$\frac{1}{2}$ cups chopped green bell peppers

1 tablespoon chopped garlic

1 (10-ounce) can of Rotel tomatoes

1 (28-ounce) can of diced tomatoes

2 bay leaves

$\frac{1}{2}$ teaspoon oregano

$\frac{1}{2}$ teaspoon thyme

$\frac{1}{2}$ teaspoon red pepper flakes

$\frac{1}{2}$ teaspoon salt

$\frac{1}{2}$ teaspoon McCormick Coarse Ground Black Pepper

8 cups chicken stock

2 cups long-grain white rice

$\frac{1}{2}$ cup chopped parsley and 1 cup chopped scallions
   (white and green parts) for garnish

The night before the tailgate, pack the bacon drippings in a sealable container. Pack the seasoned chicken thighs and andouille in separate sealable containers. Place the onions, celery, and peppers in a sealable container. Place the garlic in a sealable container. Place the Rotel and diced tomatoes in a sealable container. Place the chicken stock in a sealable container. Pack the parsley and scallions for garnish in a sealable container. Refrigerate these containers overnight and transport to the tailgate in a cooler. Pack the bay leaves, oregano, thyme, red pepper flakes, salt, and pepper in a sealable container. Pack the rice in a sealable container.

At the tailgate, prepare the jambalaya. In a large, heavy pot over a propane burner, melt the bacon drippings over medium-high heat. Add the seasoned chicken thighs. Brown on each side and remove. Set aside in a bowl. The thighs don't have to be cooked through; this step is to develop flavor in the pot and on the thighs.

Add the andouille to the pot. Stir frequently until the sausage begins to brown. Reduce heat to medium. Add the onions, celery, and peppers and stir. Cook until the onions are translucent. Add the garlic and stir.

Add the chicken thighs back to pot. Add the spices and stir. Add the tomatoes and stir. Pour in the chicken stock and bring the jambalaya to a strong simmer. Cook at a simmer for 1½ hours. Remove the bay leaves. You can turn off the heat and hold the jambalaya covered for a few hours at this point.

About 20 minutes before you want to serve the dish, bring the contents of the pot to a boil. Add the rice and reduce to a low simmer. Cover and cook for 20 minutes. Once the rice has cooked, remove the lid and stir. Garnish with parsley and scallions and serve.

Shrimp, Tasso, and Smoked Chicken Gumbo

A gumbo can be made with a variety of ingredients, from chicken and sausage to beef and seafood. The roux is what gives this gumbo its delicious nutty flavor and rich brown coloring. To make this gumbo on-site from start to finish, you need to bring a tall heavy-bottomed pot and an even taller balloon whisk.

MAKES 10–12 SERVINGS

½ cup peanut oil
½ cup all-purpose flour
3 cups chopped yellow onions
3 cups chopped green bell peppers
2 cups chopped celery
3 tablespoons chopped garlic
2 large bay leaves
3 cups diced Smoked Beer-Can Chicken (page 150) or cooked chicken
2 cups diced Tasso ham
3 pounds large shrimp, peeled, deveined, and tails removed
3 (32-ounce) boxes of chicken stock
1 (28-ounce) can of good-quality diced tomatoes
2 tablespoons Worcestershire sauce
2 teaspoons thyme
1½ teaspoons McCormick Coarse Ground Black Pepper
1 teaspoon cayenne pepper
1 teaspoon dried oregano
1 teaspoon chervil
1 tablespoon kosher salt
Chopped scallions for garnish
Tailgating Rice (page 165) for serving

The night before the tailgate, place the peanut oil in a sealable container. Place the flour in a sealable container. Place the onions, peppers, and celery in a sealable container. Place the garlic and bay leaves in a sealable container. Place the chicken and Tasso in a sealable container. Store the shrimp in a sealable container. Place the thyme, black pepper, cayenne pepper, oregano, chervil, and salt in a sealable container. Place the scallions in a sealable container. Refrigerate the containers of vegetables and meat overnight and transfer in a cooler to your tailgate.

It's easiest to prepare this dish with two burners. It will come in handy for making the rice.

Start by making the roux. There are two options. If you're an experienced cook, you can make it in 15 minutes of constant attention and stirring. If you prefer a more leisurely method, follow the 30-minute approach. The ingredients and methods are the same in both approaches; the only difference is the heat of the burner.

For the 15-minute approach, start with the pot on medium-high heat. Add the oil followed by the flour and stir constantly for 5 minutes. Reduce heat to medium and continue stirring for an additional 5 minutes. Reduce heat to low and continue stirring for 5 more minutes.

For the 30-minute method, start with the pot on medium heat. Add the oil and let it heat for 1 minute. Add the flour and stir frequently for 15 minutes. Reduce heat to low and continue stirring frequently for 15 minutes.

In both approaches, you do not want to burn the roux. If it smells like burnt popcorn, throw it out and start over. The end result in both methods should be a smooth, mahogany-colored roux.

After the roux is made, add the onions, peppers, and celery and stir. Increase heat to medium. Add the garlic and bay leaves and stir. Add the chicken and Tasso and stir. Add the chicken stock and tomatoes and stir. Add the Worcestershire and spices and stir. Bring to a simmer and cook, uncovered, for 1½ hours, stirring occasionally. Remove the bay leaves and turn the heat to low.

About 30 minutes before you're ready to eat, make the Tailgating Rice (page 165). Just before you're ready to serve, with the gumbo on low, add the shrimp and stir. Cook the shrimp until they are no longer opaque. Serve over the rice. Garnish with scallions.

Shrimp, Tasso, and
Smoked Chicken Gumbo

Sweet Potato and Three-Bean Chili

With sweet potatoes and three types of beans, this vegetarian chili proves that you won't miss the meat. To allow the flavors to develop fully, make this chili the night before the tailgate. Try serving it with toasted Sharp Cheddar Beer Bread (page 117) for a hearty late-season meal.

MAKES 10–12 SERVINGS

¼ cup corn oil
1¼ cups diced yellow onions
2½ cups peeled and diced sweet potatoes
1 cup chopped celery
1 cup chopped green bell peppers
¾ cup chopped poblano peppers
2 tablespoons chopped garlic
3 tablespoons ground cumin
3 tablespoons chili powder
2 teaspoons salt
¾ teaspoon McCormick Coarse Ground Black Pepper
1 tablespoon dark brown sugar
1 (10-ounce) can of Rotel tomatoes
1 (28-ounce) can of diced tomatoes
1 (28-ounce) can of crushed tomatoes
1 (19-ounce) can of cannellini beans, drained
1 (15½-ounce) can of navy beans, drained
2 (15½-ounce) cans of light red kidney beans, drained
1 (12-ounce) can of pale ale

Put the oil in a large stockpot and heat to medium-high. Add the onions and sweet potatoes. Stirring frequently, cook until the onions are soft and the sweet potatoes begin to brown. Reduce heat to medium.

Add the celery, peppers, and garlic. Cook for 5 minutes over medium heat, stirring occasionally.

Add the cumin and chili powder and mix well. Stir in the salt, pepper, and brown sugar. Add the tomatoes and mix well. Stir in the beans. Add the beer and stir.

Reduce heat to medium-low and cook for 1½ hours, stirring occasionally, until the sweet potatoes are tender and the chili has thickened. Let cool and refrigerate overnight in a sealable container. Transport to your tailgate in a cooler. Reheat in a slow cooker or over a burner.

Brunswick Stew

There are countless versions of Brunswick stew. I've seen Brunswick stew in small slow cookers and in twenty-gallon vats. This rendition is easy and fun to make.

MAKES 10–12 SERVINGS

3 tablespoons bacon drippings
1 cup chopped yellow onions
2 (28-ounce) cans of high-quality whole tomatoes
1 (14 $\frac{7}{10}$-ounce) can of creamed corn
2 tablespoons Worcestershire sauce
1 tablespoon red pepper flakes
4 cups peeled and diced potatoes
6 cups good-quality chicken stock, divided
4 cups chopped smoked pork shoulder
4 cups chopped smoked chicken
2 (15 ¼-ounce) cans of lima beans, drained
2 (15 ½-ounce) cans of white sweet corn, drained
1 tablespoon Tabasco sauce

Put the bacon drippings and onions in a sealable container. Pack the cans of whole tomatoes. Open the can of creamed corn and put in a container with the Worcestershire and red pepper flakes. Put the potatoes in a sealable container with 4 cups of the chicken stock. Put the smoked pork and smoked chicken in a sealable container. Put the remaining 2 cups of the chicken stock, lima beans, white corn, and Tabasco in a sealable container. Refrigerate all the containers overnight and transport in a cooler to your tailgate.

At the tailgate, place a large heavy-bottomed pot on a single propane burner. Turn heat to medium. Add the bacon drippings and onions. Cook, stirring, until the onions turn translucent. Add the whole tomatoes and stir. Add the creamed corn, Worcestershire, and red pepper flakes. Cook over medium heat for about 45 minutes, stirring occasionally. Add the potatoes and 4 cups of chicken stock. Bring to a low simmer and cook for 20 more minutes, stirring occasionally. Add the chopped pork and chicken and stir. Add the chicken stock, beans, corn, and Tabasco. Let the stew simmer for 2 hours, stirring occasionally. Keep it on low heat throughout the tailgate and let guests fill up a bowl whenever they come by.

Sandwiches have been and always will be the go-to food for tailgaters. They go beyond hamburgers and hot dogs. Anything you can cook, bake, boil, fry, or grill can be made into a sandwich. These are some of my favorite tailgating sandwiches.

Sandwiches & Soups

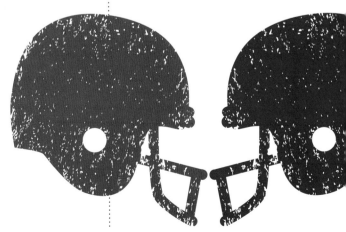

Tailgate Burger Bar

Tailgate Burger Bar

Burgers are a staple of tailgates everywhere. A homemade patty cooked up over a hot grill is hard to resist. Topping possibilities for burgers seem limitless, but there's something said for keeping it simple. All you need is the Tailgate Burger, buttered buns, lettuce, tomato, cheese, and maybe a pickle slice or two.

MAKES 8 SERVINGS

1¼ pounds ground sirloin
1¼ pounds ground round
2 tablespoons grated yellow onions
1 teaspoon Worcestershire sauce
2 teaspoons salt
¼ teaspoon black pepper
¼ teaspoon Tabasco sauce
4 tablespoons unsalted butter, softened
8 buns
8 slices of your favorite cheese (optional)
Lettuce, tomatoes, and pickles for garnish

The night before the tailgate, place the ground sirloin and the ground round in a large bowl. Sprinkle with the onions, Worcestershire, salt, pepper, and Tabasco. Using your hands, mix all the ingredients together and form the mixture into eight equally sized patties. Stack the patties with waxed paper in between each. Store in a sealable container and refrigerate. Transport to your tailgate in a cooler.

At the tailgate, grill the patties to desired doneness. While the patties are cooking, spread an even layer of butter on the cut-side of each bun half. When there's room on the grill, lay the buns down on the hot grill and toast them. Allow guests to assemble their burgers however they like best.

Wedge Sandwich

With a little bit of prep work and imagination, you can make any meal suitable for tailgating. Take, for example, the wedge salad. This classic steakhouse salad contains blue cheese, bacon, and tomatoes on top of a thick wedge of iceberg lettuce. The following is a tailgating version of the wedge salad. If you're serving a large crowd, it's easy to make these in an assembly line. The blue cheese dressing can be used for many more items than the Wedge Sandwich. Its creamy texture and bold flavor make it perfect as a dipping sauce for Clifton's Tenders (page 139), fried pickles (page 85), or a tray of celery and carrot slices.

MAKES 1 SANDWICH

Blue Cheese Dressing (makes about 5 cups)
12 ounces blue cheese, crumbled
1 cup sour cream
$\frac{1}{2}$ cup mayonnaise
2 $\frac{1}{2}$ tablespoons lemon juice
1 teaspoon Worcestershire sauce
$\frac{1}{2}$ teaspoon Tabasco sauce
$\frac{3}{4}$ teaspoon salt
$\frac{1}{2}$ teaspoon McCormick Coarse Ground Black Pepper
2 tablespoons heavy whipping cream

Sandwich
Blue cheese dressing
1 bun
$\frac{1}{2}$-inch-thick slice of iceberg lettuce
3 slices of bacon, cooked crisp
Spoonful of Blistered Grape Tomatoes (page 99)

To make the dressing, reserve 6 ounces of the blue cheese crumbles in a small bowl. Add the remaining 6 ounces of blue cheese crumbles to the bowl of a food processor. Add the rest of the dressing ingredients and process until smooth. Pour the dressing into a serving bowl and fold in the remaining 6 ounces of blue cheese crumbles. Cover and refrigerate overnight. Transport the dressing to your tailgate in a cooler.

To assemble the sandwich, spread a layer of dressing on the top and bottom halves of the bun. Place the lettuce on the bottom half. Add the bacon, the Blistered Grape Tomatoes, and then the top of the bun.

Pimento Cheese Club

Filled with smoked turkey, Virginia ham, crisp apples, and creamy pimento cheese, this sandwich is a change of pace from a traditional club. Leftover pimento cheese can make a great snack when spread on crackers or apple slices.

MAKES 1 SANDWICH

Pimento Cheese (makes about 2 cups)
8 ounces grated cheddar cheese
1 (4-ounce) jar of chopped pimentos, drained
$\frac{1}{2}$ cup mayonnaise
1 tablespoon lemon juice
1 teaspoon Worcestershire sauce
1 teaspoon grated onions
$\frac{1}{4}$ teaspoon dry mustard
$\frac{1}{4}$ teaspoon Tabasco sauce

Sandwich
3 tablespoons pimento cheese
3 slices of white sandwich bread
Red-tipped romaine lettuce
2 ounces shaved smoked turkey
2 ounces shaved Virginia ham
$\frac{1}{4}$ of a Fuji apple, thinly sliced and dipped in lemon juice
McCormick Coarse Ground Black Pepper

Add the cheddar cheese to a medium-sized bowl. Firmly press the pimentos between two layers of paper towels to remove the excess liquid, then add to the bowl of cheese. Add the mayonnaise, lemon juice, Worcestershire, onions, mustard, and Tabasco. With a fork, mix all the ingredients together until well blended. Store in a sealable container and refrigerate until ready to use.

To assemble the club, spread a layer of pimento cheese on a slice of bread. Add the lettuce and turkey. Spread pimento cheese on the second slice of bread and place it cheese-side up on the turkey. Then add the ham, apple slices, a sprinkling of pepper, and more lettuce. Spread pimento cheese on the third slice of bread and place it cheese-side down on top of the sandwich.

Cut the club into triangles before serving. If you want to assemble several of these sandwiches at home and transport them to your tailgate in a cooler, place them on a baking sheet, cover them with a slightly damp paper towel, and cover the baking sheet with plastic wrap.

Sandwich Chili

A smooth, beanless chili is a versatile topping. You can add it, along with slaw, to a "Carolina-style" burger. Add it to a hot dog, and you have a chili dog. In parts of Kentucky, you'll find a sandwich of just chili and a bun, which is known as a "chili bun." When serving chili buns as a main dish, offer grated sharp cheddar, onions, and Creamy Coleslaw (page 113) as garnishes. This recipe can be measured out the night before and cooked at your tailgate, or it can be made a day earlier and warmed up at your tailgate.

MAKES ABOUT 7 CUPS

1 tablespoon bacon drippings

2½ pounds ground sirloin

2 cups finely chopped yellow onions

3 tablespoons finely minced garlic

1 (4-ounce) jar of chopped pimentos, drained

3 tablespoons chili powder

1 teaspoon cumin

1 teaspoon dried oregano

$\frac{1}{2}$ teaspoon thyme

$\frac{1}{2}$ teaspoon ground coriander

2 teaspoons dry mustard

1$\frac{1}{2}$ teaspoons salt

1 tablespoon hot Hungarian paprika

3 cups chicken stock

1 (6-ounce) can of tomato paste

2 tablespoons unsulphured molasses
   (like Grandma's Original)

2 tablespoons lemon juice

2 tablespoons Worcestershire sauce

In a large, heavy pot over medium heat, warm the bacon drippings. Add the ground sirloin and cook. While the sirloin is cooking, break it into small pieces. Once the meat has browned, add the onions, garlic, and pimentos. Continue to cook the ground sirloin until all liquid evaporates. To help, push all the contents of the pot up against the sides, creating a ring with an empty center. The liquid will flow into the middle. Cook the mixture until the liquid has evaporated, taking care not to burn the meat.

Once the liquid has evaporated, reduce the heat to medium-low and add the chili powder, cumin, oregano, thyme, coriander, mustard, salt, and paprika. Stir together and cook for a minute. Add the chicken stock, tomato paste, molasses, lemon juice, and Worcestershire. Bring the contents of the pot to a simmer. Let simmer uncovered for an hour, stirring occasionally.

If you're making the chili ahead of time, let it cool before refrigerating in a sealable container. Transport it in a cooler to the tailgate. At the tailgate, the chili can be reheated in a pot over a burner or in a slow cooker. Serve with a ladle so your guests can add it to hot dogs, burgers, or anything they like.

Sandwich Chili

Pregame Walks

The attachment that fans form to their undergraduate institutions is so strong that they often pass this attachment down to their children. At college football tailgates, you'll see dozens of kids dressed in pint-sized jerseys or mini cheerleader costumes. These children are being conditioned to love their parents'—and potentially their future—alma maters. Game-day tailgates are an important part of many a childhood.

For these fans-in-training, a favorite part of the tailgate happens around two and a half hours before kickoff, when the players walk to the stadium. The path and details vary at each institution, although the concept is the same. The player walks are a chance for children to see up close the player whose number they are wearing or cheerleader whose routine they are imitating. If lucky, they may even get a high-five from their favorite player. It isn't just the children who enjoy seeing the players walk to the stadium; fans of all ages make a point to see the walk.

Many of these players go on to play in professional football and become household names, but during the walk they are still students. Fans carry signs or high-five their former high school teammates or current lab partners. While taking part in Auburn's Tiger Walk, I stood next to a high school teacher. As we waited for the players to arrive, she told me stories about how, in one of her classes a few years back, she had taught a member of Auburn's defense. When the players walked by, it was pretty easy to pick out who her student had been—he stopped and greeted her with an enormous bear hug. These walks help fans and players connect personally.

Timing

Most walks take place about two or two and a half hours prior to kickoff. To secure a spot in the front row, many fans arrive thirty to forty-five minutes early. If you know that members of your tailgate want to take part in the team's walk to the stadium, set an alarm to alert them when they should head over.

Location and Length

All player walks end at the stadium, though the path often varies. In Gainesville and Tuscaloosa, the walks consist of short paths right to the stadium. The Ole Miss, Starkville, and West Virginia paths cut through tailgating areas. Setting up your tailgate along the path the football players walk will bring quite a crowd.

Team Spirit

Player walks are pure school spirit. They can be named after a mascot, like Richmond's "Spider Walk," Duke's "Devil Walk," or Georgia's "Dawg Walk." Or they can stand for an ideal—the walks at Ole Miss and Alabama are known as the "Walk of Champions."

Most walks include players and coaches, cheerleaders, bands, and costumed mascots. Some schools have special guests lead the way. In Baton Rouge, Mike, the university's live Bengal tiger, takes part in LSU's March Down the Hill. During the Vol Walk, Smokey, Tennessee's bluetick coonhound, leads the way. In Atlanta, it isn't a live animal leading the players to the stadium but the "Ramblin' Wreck," Georgia Tech's prized gold 1930 Ford Cabriolet Sport Coupe.

Universities have recognized the popularity and success of player walks. If your team doesn't have one yet, there's a good chance that it will soon. In 2011, I experienced a walk during West Virginia's inaugural season. Mountaineer fans were incredibly receptive to this new tradition that head coach Dana Holgorsen implemented in his first season. Thousands gathered on either side of a path leading up to the stadium as the players made their way through the Blue Lot toward the stadium entrance. In recognition of West Virginia's coal mining heritage, the walk was named the "Mountaineer Mantrip." A man-trip is the name of the car that takes miners deep into the mines. At the walk's end, players entered the stadium and rubbed a large block of coal to remember those who lost their lives in the Upper Big Branch Mine collapse.

With the band playing, thousands cheering, and a sea of school colors, player walks are an exciting part of many pregame traditions. If you've never taken part in your favorite team's player walk, I encourage you to do so. It's a great part of any game day. ■

Georgia fans and players during the Dawg Walk

Fried Shrimp Sandwich with
Tangy Citrus Sauce

Fried Shrimp Sandwiches with Tangy Citrus Sauce

Sweet fried shrimp, crusty French bread, roasted grape tomatoes, crisp lettuce, and a drizzle of a Tangy Citrus Sauce. This is what I think a fried shrimp sandwich should be.

MAKES 6 SANDWICHES

Tangy Citrus Sauce (makes about 1 cup)

1 cup mayonnaise

1 tablespoon fresh lemon juice

½ teaspoon Creole mustard

½ teaspoon grated lime zest

½ teaspoon grated lemon zest

¼ teaspoon salt

¼ teaspoon sugar

¼ teaspoon Tabasco sauce

¼ teaspoon Worcestershire sauce

⅛ teaspoon paprika

⅛ teaspoon black pepper

Fried Shrimp

2 pounds (21–25 count) shrimp, peeled and deveined

2 cups self-rising flour

1 cup self-rising yellow cornmeal

1½ teaspoons salt (plus extra for seasoning)

½ teaspoon McCormick Coarse Ground Black Pepper
 (plus extra for seasoning)

¼ teaspoon cayenne pepper

¼ teaspoon garlic powder

Peanut oil for frying

Sandwich

2 loaves of French bread, cut into thirds

12 leaves of romaine lettuce, washed

Fried shrimp

Blistered Grape Tomatoes (page 99)

Tangy Citrus Sauce

The night before the tailgate, add all the sauce ingredients to a bowl and stir until evenly mixed together. Store in a sealable container and refrigerate. Place the shrimp in a sealable container and refrigerate. In a sealable plastic bag, mix together the flour, cornmeal, salt, black pepper, cayenne pepper, and garlic powder. Transfer the refrigerated containers in a cooler to your tailgate.

At the tailgate, season the shrimp to taste with salt and pepper. Add the shrimp to the bag of dredge and shake to cover. Fry the coated shrimp in small batches in 365° oil until golden brown. Place the shrimp on a sheet pan lined with paper towels or paper bags.

Open the six pieces of French bread. Line each sandwich with two leaves of romaine. Put ⅓ of a pound of fried shrimp in each sandwich. Top each sandwich with a generous spoonful of Blistered Grape Tomatoes. Drizzle with Tangy Citrus Sauce and serve immediately.

A Reason to Leave Your Tailgate

Advancements in technology have changed tailgating. The accessibility of generators, flat-screen TVs, and portable satellite receivers allows tailgaters to watch the game on-site and in the comfort of their tailgate. For many tailgaters, being able to stay with their food and drink while still being surrounded by the magic of a college campus on game day is the ideal situation.

However, there's one thing that TV can't re-create. If you're actually inside the stadium, you're surrounded by thousands of fellow fans. As the anticipation builds, so does the volume. Not a soul is sitting. Everyone is waiting anxiously for the game to start. The suspense is so intense, you can practically feel it in the air. On the Jumbotron, a video plays filled with past game highlights and commentary from current players, bringing every fan to his or her feet. Then it happens: cannons boom, fireworks are released, and the players come rushing through the tunnel and onto the field.

Every school plans an exciting entrance, but some take their entrances above and beyond a Jumbotron and fireworks in a variety of ways. At Texas Tech, ever since he first appeared at the 1954 Gator Bowl, the Masked Rider, sitting atop a black quarter horse, has led the Red Raiders onto the field. In homage to the state's early settlers, the Oklahoma football team is led onto the field by a conestoga wagon known as the Sooner Schooner. Pulling the wagon are two white ponies, Boomer and Sooner. The most famous 1930 Ford Cabriolet Sport Coupe in existence leads Georgia Tech onto the field. On game day,

it carries in the cheerleaders and leads the football team to the stadium. Then, prior to kickoff, the classic car goes first as the team runs onto the field. For over fifty years, fans have cheered as the "Ramblin' Wreck" leads Georgia Tech's Yellow Jackets on their way to victory.

Since the 1950s, the Miami Hurricanes have entered the field by running through a thick cloud of white smoke. The purple and gold East Carolina Pirates have a similar entrance, but their smoke incorporates their school's colors. As the Pirates prepare to take the field, fans watch as thick purple smoke rolls out of the skull-shaped tunnel. With Jimi Hendrix's "Purple Haze" playing and cannons firing, the Pirates charge onto the field.

On my visits to Blacksburg, Virginia, and Columbia, South Carolina, I noticed certain special songs being played throughout the day. At Virginia Tech, fans go crazy whenever they hear Metallica's "Enter Sandman." In South Carolina, fans have an unexplainable bond with Richard Strauss's "Also Sprach Zarathustra," more commonly known as the opening theme from *2001: A Space Odyssey*. If you're a Hokie or Gamecock fan, you know exactly what these songs mean, and the songs and the entrances they represent resonate throughout the tailgate.

Here are some of my favorite college game-day entrances.

Clemson: Running Down the Hill

Every Clemson fan can watch the team enter Memorial Stadium. You don't need a game ticket to take part. Before the west end zone expansion was added, Clemson players suited up in Fike Field House and ran down the east end zone hill into the stadium. Now, the team members

Clemson Players getting ready to run down the hill

dress in the west end zone locker room, board a bus, and are driven around the outside of the stadium to the east end zone. As the players file out of the bus, hundreds of fans are lined up outside the stadium to cheer them on. When the announcer says, "Your Clemson Tigers!" a cannon fires, the band plays the "Tiger Rag," and, as the more than 80,000 fans cheer, each team member touches Howard's Rock and sprints down the hill and onto the field. In touching Howard's Rock, Clemson players are pledging to give 110 percent. On game day, I found several Clemson fans who had created replicas of this rock for themselves. Like the players taking the field, these fans promised to give 110 percent in their tailgating.

Florida State:
Chief Osceola and Renegade

Florida State is the only team whose mascot, Chief Osceola, leads players onto the field while wielding a flaming spear. Atop his Appaloosa, Renegade, and as the more than 80,000 fans join in the war chant and make a tomahawk hand signal, Chief Osceola rides around the field while the Florida State players run to the sidelines. After the players have lined up, the chief rides to midfield, where he hurtles the flaming spear into the ground. The crowd's chant then erupts into a bellowing cheer, and Florida State is ready to take on its opponent.

Texas A&M: Twelfth Man Entrance

In 1922, when Texas A&M was running out of players during a game, E. King Gill answered his team's call. He left the stands, suited up, and stood on the sidelines, ready to play. Little did he know that his actions would become a part of Texas A&M tradition. The spirit of his gesture, the desire to help his team when it was in need, has become known throughout Aggieland as the "Twelfth Man." When the eleven men on the field needed him, he was there. Texas A&M's student body and alumni have adopted this idea by calling themselves the Twelfth Man, too. Organized by Yell Leaders, students stand and cheer for their team throughout the whole game. The Corps of Cadets lead the players onto the field from outside the stadium. The crowd hears the drummers' cadence and erupts in cheers as the band and team appear. Being a part of the Twelfth Man tradition is something every Aggie fan relishes, and when they tailgate, Texas A&M fans tailgate as the Twelfth Man.

Auburn: War Eagle

On game day, Auburn's battle cry of "War Eagle" can be heard everywhere on campus. It's a common salutation among Auburn fans, and there are varying legends about its origins. One of them involves an incident in 1892 at the first Auburn-Georgia game. At the game, an Auburn alumnus's pet eagle escaped and began circling the field. Auburn won the game, and the "War Eagle" tradition began. Over the decades, the tradition has evolved, and now, before every home game, an eagle flies from the top of the stadium and lands in the center of the field. As the eagle begins to soar, the crowd yells "Warrrrrrrrrrrrr . . ." and as the eagle lands, "Eagle!"

Tennessee: Running through the "T"

Tennessee's letter "T" is everywhere on game day. From cakes to cornhole boards, Vols fans will put the letter on anything they can. This single letter is iconic to Tennessee fans. Inside the stadium, you'll see the largest "T," because the Tennessee Volunteers football team makes its entrance with the help of the Pride of the Southland Band. Dating back to 1964, the band has performed on the field before the players arrive. At the end of the field show, the band forms a T next to the end zone, and to the cheers of over 100,000 fans, the Volunteers run through this T-formation and over to their sideline. ■

Crab Cake Sliders

Sliders are a good size for game day. If you just want a taste, you can eat one. If you're looking for a whole meal, you can put several on your plate. Sliders are versatile, but my favorite type is a delicious crab cake on a buttery bun with a squeeze of lemon.

MAKES 8 SLIDERS

1 pound lump crabmeat, picked through to remove any bits of shell
8 unsalted soda crackers, crumbled
3 tablespoons Tangy Citrus Sauce (page 185)
1 large egg
1 tablespoon mayonnaise
1 tablespoon finely diced red bell peppers
1 tablespoon finely diced yellow bell peppers
1 tablespoon finely diced green bell peppers
$\frac{1}{2}$ teaspoon Creole mustard
$\frac{1}{4}$ teaspoon minced garlic
$\frac{1}{4}$ teaspoon salt
$\frac{1}{4}$ teaspoon Worcestershire sauce
$\frac{1}{8}$ teaspoon black pepper
$\frac{1}{8}$ teaspoon Tabasco sauce
4 tablespoons unsalted butter (for frying)
Buttered slider buns
Lemon wedges for garnish

Place the crabmeat in a medium bowl and set aside. In a small bowl, put the crumbled crackers, Tangy Citrus Sauce, egg, mayonnaise, peppers, mustard, garlic, salt, Worcestershire, pepper, and Tabasco. Mix with a fork until all the ingredients are well blended. Pour the mixture over the crabmeat and gently toss the crabmeat in the mixture until well blended. Form into 8 crab cakes. Place on a pan or plate, cover with plastic wrap, and refrigerate overnight. Transport in a cooler to your tailgate.

At the tailgate, melt 2 tablespoons of the butter in a frying pan over a burner on medium heat. Place four of the crab cakes in the pan. Cook on both sides until golden brown. Turn heat to low and cook for an additional 4 minutes. Serve on buttered slider buns with a wedge of lemon. Repeat the process with the 4 remaining crab cakes.

Crab Cake Sliders

Grown-Up Grilled Cheese with Cognac Mustard Butter

On cold days, there's nothing like a hot grilled cheese sandwich and a bowl of soup. Soup and sandwiches are a great tailgating combination. Serve your soup in a mug so your guests can easily dunk their sandwiches. This Grown-Up Grilled Cheese is one of my favorites.

MAKES 1 SANDWICH

Cognac Mustard Butter (makes about 1½ cups)
10 tablespoons unsalted butter, softened
⅓ cup spicy brown mustard
1 tablespoon honey
1 tablespoon Cognac
1 tablespoon heavy whipping cream
½ teaspoon salt
½ teaspoon Tabasco sauce

Sandwich
Softened unsalted butter for grilling
Cognac Mustard Butter
2 slices marble rye bread
2–3 ounces Jarlsberg swiss cheese, sliced thin
3 thin shallot slices
2 slices of thick-cut applewood bacon, cooked crisp

To make the butter, add all the ingredients to the bowl of a food processor. Process until blended. Transfer to a sealable container and refrigerate until ready to use.

Spread unsalted butter on the outside of both slices of bread and Cognac Mustard Butter on the inside. Lay the sliced cheese, shallots, and bacon on the bottom slice. Add another layer of sliced cheese on top of the bacon and then the top slice of bread. Put the sandwich on a hot griddle. Cook until the bottom has browned and the cheese begins to melt. Flip the sandwich. Press with a spatula and cook until the other side is browned. Remove from the griddle. Cut in half and enjoy with Cream of Tomato Soup (page 193) or Creamy Carrot and Sweet Potato Soup (page 194).

Cream of Tomato Soup, Creamy Carrot and Sweet
Potato Soup (p. 194), and Grown-Up Grilled Cheese
with Cognac Mustard Butter (page 191)

Cream of Tomato Soup

On cold game days, there's nothing better than a hot bowl of creamy tomato soup. Its beautiful and rich red color is a perfect way for N.C. State Wolf Pack, Western Kentucky Hilltopper, or Louisville Cardinal fans to show their team spirit. It pairs perfectly with any pressed or open-faced sandwich. Making it at home and heating it on-site makes for a quick midday meal.

MAKES 8–10 SERVINGS

4 tablespoons unsalted butter

1 1/2 cups chopped yellow onions

1 tablespoon chopped garlic

4 (28-ounce) cans of high-quality diced tomatoes

2 tablespoons dark brown sugar

1/4 teaspoon dried thyme

2 teaspoons salt

1/2 teaspoon black pepper

2 cups heavy cream

1/2 teaspoon Tabasco sauce

In a large heavy-bottomed pot, melt the butter over medium heat. Add the onions and garlic. Cook until translucent and fragrant. Add the tomatoes, brown sugar, thyme, salt, and pepper. Bring to a simmer and cook for 25–30 minutes. Remove from heat. Using an immersion blender, purée the soup until smooth. If you don't have an immersion blender, you can blend the soup in several batches in a standard blender.

Once puréed, add the heavy cream and stir until blended. Add the Tabasco and stir. Let cool and refrigerate overnight in a sealable container. Transport to the tailgate in a cooler. At the tailgate, reheat on a burner or the grill.

Creamy Carrot and Sweet Potato Soup

The leaves are turning. The air is crisp. There's nothing more nourishing than a bowl of Creamy Carrot and Sweet Potato Soup. The flavors of fall in this soup complement an orange or yellow tailgating table.

MAKES 8–10 SERVINGS

6 tablespoons unsalted butter
1½ cups chopped yellow onions
¾ cup chopped leeks (white part only)
¾ cup peeled and chopped Granny Smith apples
1 pound carrots, chopped
4 cups peeled and chopped sweet potatoes
1½ teaspoons salt
½ teaspoon Chinese five-spice powder
⅛ teaspoon cayenne pepper
7 cups chicken stock
2 cups heavy cream

In a large stockpot, melt the butter. Add the onions, leeks, and apples and cook over medium heat until they soften. Add the carrots and sweet potatoes and cook over medium heat, stirring for 5 minutes. Add the salt, Chinese five-spice powder, and cayenne pepper and stir. Add the chicken stock. Cook until the carrots and sweet potatoes are fork tender. Cool for 15 minutes. Purée with an immersion blender until the soup is smooth. If you don't have an immersion blender, purée the soup in several batches in a standard blender.

Once puréed, add the heavy cream and stir until the soup is well blended. Let cool. Refrigerate overnight in a sealable container. Transport to the tailgate in a cooler. At the tailgate, reheat on a burner or the grill.

You've had a successful tailgate. Everything on your menu was a hit, and guests are happy! Well, almost all are happy. There are bound to be those guests who feel that a meal, especially a social gathering, isn't complete without dessert. Even if it's just a small "something sweet" for them to eat as they walk to the game, dessert can make a good tailgate great.

Desserts

Carrot Cake with Citrus Cream Cheese Frosting

Game day is a celebration. What celebration is complete without your favorite cake? For me, only my mom's carrot cake will do. I have it every year for my birthday and could eat it any time of day. When you're bringing your favorite cake to a tailgate, baking it in a single-layer pan allows for easy transportation. The pans that come with a raised plastic lid will prevent the icing from sticking.

MAKES 8–12 SERVINGS

Cake

4 large eggs

1 ¼ cups corn oil

1 cup dark brown sugar

1 cup granulated sugar

1 teaspoon vanilla extract

4 cups grated carrots

1 (8-ounce) can of crushed pineapple, drained

1 cup golden raisins

1 ½ cups sweetened coconut flakes

1 teaspoon grated orange zest

2 cups all-purpose flour

1 tablespoon ground cinnamon

2 teaspoons baking powder

2 teaspoons powdered ginger

1 teaspoon salt

1 teaspoon baking soda

½ teaspoon freshly grated nutmeg

Frosting

4 ounces unsalted butter, softened

6 ounces cream cheese, softened

1 teaspoon vanilla extract

1 teaspoon grated lemon zest

¾ teaspoon grated orange zest

½ teaspoon grated lime zest

Pinch of salt

3 cups confectioners' sugar

Preheat the oven to 325°.

To make the cake, place the eggs, oil, sugars, and vanilla extract in a bowl. Mix on medium speed until all the ingredients are incorporated. Add the carrots, pineapple, raisins, coconut, and orange zest. Mix on medium speed for 1 minute.

In a large bowl, stir together the flour, cinnamon, baking powder, ginger, salt, baking soda, and nutmeg. Add the flour and spice mixture in thirds to the egg and oil mixture. Mix for 30 seconds after each addition. Pour the batter into a buttered and floured 9 × 13-inch baking pan. Bake for 55 minutes or until a cake tester comes out clean. Cool the cake completely.

To make the Citrus Cream Cheese Frosting, add the butter, cream cheese, vanilla extract, citrus zest, and salt to the bowl of a mixer. Mix until the ingredients are creamed together. While mixing on low, add the confectioners' sugar in thirds, waiting for the sugar to be absorbed before adding the next third. Once all the sugar has been absorbed, mix the frosting on medium speed for 2 minutes, creating a thick and smooth icing. Remove from the mixing bowl and spread in an even layer on top of the cooled cake.

Triple Peanut Butter Cookies and Caitlin's
Cranberry Chocolate Oatmeal Cookies (p. 200)

Triple Peanut Butter Cookies

With creamy peanut butter, peanut butter chips, and salted Virginia peanuts, these cookies are a triple peanut treat. Whether you serve them at your own tailgate or bring them as a gift for your host, they'll disappear quickly from any tailgating spread.

MAKES ABOUT 48 3-INCH COOKIES

2 sticks unsalted butter, softened
1 cup granulated sugar
1 cup dark brown sugar
1 teaspoon vanilla extract
2 large eggs, beaten
1 cup creamy peanut butter
1 (16-ounce) bag of peanut butter chips
3 cups all-purpose flour
2 teaspoons baking soda
¼ teaspoon salt
1 cup chopped salted Virginia peanuts

Preheat the oven to 350°.

In a mixing bowl, add the butter, sugars, and vanilla extract. Mix on medium speed until smooth and creamy. Add the eggs, peanut butter, and peanut butter chips. Mix on low speed until all the ingredients are incorporated.

Sift the flour, baking soda, and salt into a separate bowl. Add the flour mixture to the peanut butter mixture in thirds, mixing after each addition.

Scoop out the dough with a spoon, roll into 1½-inch balls, and place on a lined baking sheet. Flatten each ball with the tines of a fork, making a crisscross pattern. Sprinkle each cookie with a few of the chopped peanuts. Bake for 10 minutes or until the cookies' edges begin to brown. Remove them from the baking sheet and let them cool on a wire rack. Store in a sealable container and set them out on your tailgating table when you're ready to serve.

Caitlin's Cranberry Chocolate Oatmeal Cookies

My sister is a huge fan of dried cranberries, almonds, and any type of chocolate. When these ingredients are combined in a cookie, you have a combination that's hard to resist. It's best to make these when no one else is around. If you don't, you'll most likely end up with only about 3 dozen to bring to your tailgate.

MAKES ABOUT 48 3-INCH COOKIES

2 sticks unsalted butter, softened
¾ cup granulated sugar
½ cup light brown sugar
2 large eggs
1½ teaspoons vanilla extract
1½ cups all-purpose flour
1 teaspoon baking soda
½ teaspoon salt
1 cup slivered almonds, toasted
1 cup dried cranberries
1 (11-ounce) bag of white chocolate chips
1 (10-ounce) bag of dark chocolate chips
2½ cups sweetened coconut flakes
2½ cups old-fashioned rolled oats

Preheat the oven to 325°.

In a large mixing bowl, cream together the butter and sugars. Beat in the eggs, one at a time, mixing after each addition. Add the vanilla extract.

In a medium-sized bowl, sift together the flour, baking soda, and salt. Add the flour mixture in thirds to the creamed butter and sugar mixture, mixing after each addition.

In a separate large bowl, add the almonds, cranberries, white and dark chocolate chips, coconut, and oats and toss. Gently fold into the cookie dough.

Form the dough into balls about 1½ inches in diameter. Place on a lined baking sheet. Flatten the cookies and bake for 18–22 minutes. The cookies are done when they begin to brown around the edges. Let the cookies cool on the baking sheet for 5 minutes before transferring to a wire rack.

Mint Chocolate Chip Bourbon Balls

October is the best month for football in Lexington, Kentucky. Home games are at night to accommodate fans' love for both their Wildcats and horse racing. Fans will tailgate for the afternoon races at Keeneland Race Track and then make their way to the stadium to tailgate for the evening's University of Kentucky football game. These Mint Chocolate Chip Bourbon Balls transform the flavors of the famous mint julep found at the spring races into a dessert made for a fall race and game day.

MAKES 18 BALLS

1 cup pecans

2 cups vanilla wafers

½ cup confectioners' sugar

2 tablespoons unsweetened cocoa powder (not Dutch-process)

2 tablespoons light corn syrup

½ cup mini chocolate chips

2 tablespoons bourbon

2 tablespoons crème de menthe

Preheat the oven to 325°.

Toast the pecans for 5–6 minutes until they are lightly browned and fragrant. Let cool. In the bowl of a food processor, pulse the vanilla wafers until they are finely ground. Add the pecans and pulse until the nuts are finely chopped.

In a large mixing bowl, mix the ground pecans and vanilla wafers with the confectioners' sugar and cocoa powder. Pour the corn syrup, chocolate chips, bourbon, and crème de menthe into the bowl. Mix with a fork until all the liquid has been absorbed and a thick dough

Mint Chocolate Chip Bourbon Balls

forms. Roll the dough between your hands into ping-pong-sized balls. Cover the bourbon balls in either confectioners' sugar or cocoa powder. Store in a sealable container and take to your tailgate. If covering in confectioners' sugar, you may want to re-roll the bourbon balls in confectioners' sugar before serving.

Training Table Brownies

When you're a child, the world seems like a bigger place. This is especially true when it comes to desserts. When my mom was little, her father was a recruiter for Duke University's football team. For home games, they would have brownies on the players' training table menu. My grandfather would always find a way to sneak home a few for my mom and my aunt Susan to eat. My mom remembers the brownies as being huge rectangles of chocolate covered in a rich, delicious chocolate icing—the biggest dessert she had ever seen.

MAKES 16–20 SERVINGS

Brownies
2 sticks plus 6 tablespoons unsalted butter
4 (1-ounce) squares of unsweetened baking chocolate
2 cups granulated sugar
1 cup light brown sugar
7 large eggs
$\frac{1}{2}$ teaspoon salt
2 teaspoons vanilla extract
$1\frac{1}{2}$ cups all-purpose flour
$\frac{3}{4}$ cups cocoa powder (not Dutch-process)
$\frac{1}{2}$ teaspoon baking powder

Frosting
1 stick unsalted butter, softened
3 cups confectioners' sugar
4–6 tablespoons heavy whipping cream
1 teaspoon vanilla extract
Pinch of salt
1 (12-ounce) bag of semisweet chocolate chips

Training Table Brownies

Preheat the oven to 325°.

To make the brownies, melt the butter in a large heavy-bottomed pot over medium heat. Reduce heat to low and add the baking chocolate. Stir until the chocolate has melted. Remove the pot from heat. Add the sugars and stir until incorporated into the butter and chocolate. Let the mixture cool for 10 minutes.

While the chocolate and sugar mixture is cooling, crack the eggs into a medium-sized bowl. Beat with a fork until the yolks and whites are mixed. Add the salt and vanilla extract to the eggs and mix. Pour the eggs into the cooled chocolate and sugar mixture and stir together.

Mix the flour, cocoa powder, and baking powder in a large bowl. Pour the flour mixture into the chocolate and egg mixture and stir until a thick batter forms.

Grease an 18 × 13-inch sheet pan with butter. Line the bottom of the sheet pan with parchment paper and grease the top of the parchment paper with butter. Lightly flour. Pour the batter onto the sheet pan and spread in an even layer. Bake for 25 minutes.

To make the frosting, place the butter in a stand mixer. Add the confectioners' sugar, 4 tablespoons of the whipping cream, the vanilla extract, and the salt. Turn the mixer to low until the sugar is incorporated, then mix on medium until a thick frosting forms. Melt the chocolate chips over a double boiler. With the mixer running on low, pour the warm melted chocolate into the frosting. Mix until all the chocolate is incorporated into the frosting. Increase the speed to medium. Beat until the frosting is fluffy, adding 1–2 tablespoons of whipping cream if needed. Immediately frost the cooled brownies. Let the frosting set on the brownies for an hour before wrapping in plastic wrap. Cut into squares prior to serving.

State Fairs and Tailgating

College football tailgating and state fairs have quite a bit in common. Both happen in the fall. Both have competitions that involve pigs, or at least pigskin. Both attract thousands of people. Tailgating and state fairs are both centered around eating and require food that can be eaten while standing up. At a tailgate, you spend most of the day on your feet, socializing with friends and visiting other tailgates. At the fair, your day is spent walking and exploring the different rides, games, and exhibits.

Unlike most states, North Carolina and South Carolina's state fairgrounds are next to college football stadiums. In Raleigh, the state fairgrounds host the tailgating lots for North Carolina State football fans. During the fair, these grounds are filled with thousands of people exploring the rides, games, and exhibitions, carrying fair food in either hand. On game day, you'll see a similar crowd. This time, though, it's tailgaters who bring the food and games.

The University of South Carolina has a similar tailgating environment. With Williams-Brice Stadium located adjacent to the fairgrounds, the parking lot that at times hosts a wide variety of rides and attractions also provides space for tailgates of all kinds. The buildings where food is judged during the fair competitions are filled with tailgaters serving up some blue-ribbon food of their own. Unfortunately, these fairgrounds aren't able to host game day and the fair at the same time. To accommodate both events, the schools play away games during the state fair.

In Texas, however, game day and the fair co-exist. Fair Park in Dallas is large enough to handle the crowds of both. Inside the fairgrounds sits Cotton Bowl Stadium. With a capacity of 92,000 people, this is one of the biggest stadiums in the country. Every year, thousands of fans head to the fairgrounds to witness the Fair Classic between Grambling State University and Prairie View A&M University and the Red River Rivalry between the University of Oklahoma and the University of Texas. The only way to get to Cotton Bowl Stadium is to walk through the fair. For this reason, many tailgaters abandon traditional tailgating and spend their pre- and postgame time at the fair.

I was at the 2010 Red River Rivalry and witnessed a game-day atmosphere unlike any other. This annual matchup between the Texas Longhorns and Oklahoma Sooners is on every Texas and Oklahoma fan's calendar. Austin and Norman are around three hours apart on I-35. From Thursday night through Sunday, thousands of fans arrive to take over Dallas for this yearly showdown. Every hotel, restaurant, and bar is filled with Longhorn burnt orange and Sooner crimson.

I was used to seeing thousands of people congregating outside a football stadium on grass lawns and in parking lots and tailgaters parking their cars, setting up tents, and firing up their grills, but what I experienced at the Red River Rivalry was in no way what I was used to seeing. With the stadium inside the fairgrounds, most of the 92,000 fans holding a game ticket spent their pregame time riding rides, eating funnel cakes, and playing games. The food they were eating was not normal tailgate fare but included fried butter, funnel cakes, deep-fried cookie dough, deep-fried bacon, and, of course, the famous Texas State Fair Corny Dog.

Because it's a neutral-site game, everyone in attendance wore their pride for their team. Once the Cotton Bowl had filled and the game

Texas and Oklahoma fans at Fair Park for the Red River Rivalry in Dallas

had begun, there were still thousands of Oklahoma and Texas fans outside the stadium on the fairgrounds, all there to celebrate, cheer on their team, and, of course, enjoy the fair. It just goes to show that great rivalries and passionate fan bases know no bounds. The spirit of tailgating is alive and well when these two teams get together, even if the setting is not one you would find on a typical game day. ■

Mini Funnel Cakes

Mini Funnel Cakes

A trip to the state fair isn't complete without a funnel cake. When you're tailgating on the fairgrounds, it makes sense to end your tailgate with this treat. Using a squeeze bottle and a pastry ring, you can make your own Mini Funnel Cakes.

MAKES 15–20 4-INCH CAKES

1½ cups all-purpose flour
¼ cup confectioners' sugar
1 teaspoon baking powder
¼ teaspoon salt
1⅓ cups milk
½ teaspoon vanilla extract
¼ teaspoon grated lemon zest
1 egg
Peanut oil for frying
Confectioners' sugar for garnish

The night before the tailgate, measure out the flour, sugar, baking powder, and salt. Pack in a sealable container. Add the milk, vanilla extract, grated lemon zest, and egg to a separate sealable container; refrigerate overnight and transfer to your tailgate in a cooler.

Bring a plastic squeeze bottle, a shallow frying pan, a 4-inch metal pastry ring, and tongs to the tailgate.

At the tailgate, add the flour mixture to a medium-sized bowl with a lipped rim and mix together. Pour in the milk mixture and stir together, creating a thick batter. Slowly pour the batter into the squeeze bottle.

Place a large, shallow frying pan on a propane burner. Pour in about a ½ inch of the oil and heat to 350°. Place the metal pastry ring into the pan. Squeeze the batter from the bottle into the ring, moving the bottle back and forth and connecting pieces of dough in a zigzag pattern. Cook for about 45 seconds. With tongs, remove the metal ring and flip the funnel cake. Cook on the opposite side for about 45 more seconds, until light brown in color.

Use the first few cakes as an experiment to figure out the cooking time and squeezing pattern that suit your tastes. Top the hot funnel cakes with powdered sugar, Raspberry Syrup (page 35), Blackberry Syrup (page 37), or your favorite chocolate sauce. Serve on a square piece of wax paper so your guests can hold a funnel cake in one hand. The funnel cakes are best eaten when warm and made to order.

Deep-Fried Cookie Dough

From bacon to butter, if it can be battered, it will be deep-fried and served at the state fair. Texas and Oklahoma fans might disagree about which team to cheer for, but I saw both sides enjoying fried desserts before kickoff of the Red River Rivalry. Of all the fried foods, my favorite is fried cookie dough. This eggless cookie dough is ideal for eating unbaked. Making the dough and rolling it into balls ahead of time will allow you to quickly fry it up on-site. There's a bit of technique you'll need to develop to coat the dough fully in the wash and dredge, so I recommend trying this recipe out at home before taking it to your tailgate.

MAKES 8 SERVINGS

$\frac{1}{2}$ cup all-purpose flour

$\frac{1}{4}$ teaspoon salt

4 tablespoons unsalted butter, softened

$\frac{1}{4}$ cup light brown sugar

3 tablespoons granulated sugar

$\frac{1}{4}$ teaspoon vanilla extract

2 tablespoons vegetable oil, divided

$\frac{1}{4}$ cup chocolate chips

1 cup milk

1 egg

$1\frac{1}{4}$ cups self-rising flour

2 tablespoons confectioners' sugar

Peanut oil for frying

Confectioners' sugar and chocolate syrup for garnish

Deep-Fried Cookie Dough

Make the dough the night before the tailgate. In a small bowl, mix together the flour and salt. In a mixing bowl, cream together the butter and sugars. While mixing, add the vanilla extract and 1 tablespoon of the oil. Continue mixing the dough while slowly adding the flour mixture. Add the remaining tablespoon of oil. Mix in the chocolate chips. Remove the dough from the bowl and form into 8 evenly sized balls. Store in a sealable container and refrigerate overnight. In a separate sealable container, add the milk and egg and refrigerate overnight. In an additional sealable container, add the flour and confectioners' sugar. Transport the refrigerated containers in a cooler to your tailgate.

When you're ready to fry the cookie dough, stir the milk mixture, then dip the cookie dough in it. Roll it in the flour mixture, dip it back into the milk mixture, and then roll it in the flour mixture again. Repeat this process a total of 3 times, until a thick coating has formed around the dough. Make sure the dough is entirely coated.

Fill a Dutch oven ⅔ of the way full with oil and heat over a propane burner to 365°. Fry the battered balls of cookie dough for 1½–2 minutes until golden brown on the outside. Remove from the oil and drain on paper bags. Serve the Deep-Fried Cookie Dough with confectioners' sugar and your favorite chocolate syrup.

Apple Crisp with Bourbon Whipped Cream

There are no rivalries when it comes to our love of apple pie. It's American comfort food. Apple Crisp with Bourbon Whipped Cream is a great way to wind up your successful tailgating season. Bake the crisp the day before or the morning of the tailgate.

MAKES 10–12 SERVINGS

Streusel
2 sticks unsalted butter, melted
1 teaspoon vanilla extract
½ teaspoon almond extract
2½ cups all-purpose flour
¾ cup granulated sugar
¼ cup light brown sugar
½ teaspoon salt
½ teaspoon freshly grated nutmeg

Filling
4 tablespoons fresh lemon juice
4 cups Fuji apples, peeled and chopped into bite-sized pieces
4 cups Gala apples, peeled and chopped into bite-sized pieces
4 cups Granny Smith apples, peeled and chopped into
   bite-sized pieces
4 tablespoons unsalted butter, melted
½ cup granulated sugar
3 tablespoons all-purpose flour
½ teaspoon ground cinnamon
¼ teaspoon salt

Bourbon Whipped Cream
1 pint heavy whipping cream, chilled
2 tablespoons bourbon
1 teaspoon vanilla extract
½ cup confectioners' sugar
Pinch of salt

Apple Crisp with Bourbon Whipped Cream

Preheat the oven to 350°.

To make the streusel topping, combine the melted butter, vanilla extract, and almond extract in a small bowl. In a medium-sized bowl, mix together the flour, sugars, salt, and nutmeg. Pour the melted butter mixture into the flour mixture. Mix with a fork until completely blended. Set aside.

Prepare the apple filling. Add the lemon juice to a large bowl. As you peel and chop the apples, add them to the bowl of lemon juice. Add the 4 tablespoons melted butter and toss.

In a small bowl, mix together the sugar, flour, cinnamon, and salt. Pour this flour mixture into the bowl of apples. Stir, coating the apples evenly in the butter and flour mixture. Butter an 11¾ × 9½-inch disposable aluminum lasagna pan. Pour the apple filling into the pan.

Crumble the streusel mixture in an even layer over the apple filling. Bake for 40–45 minutes. Remove the crisp from the oven and let it cool. Once it's completely cool, cover and refrigerate.

The night before the tailgate, place the whipping cream, bourbon, and vanilla extract in a sealable container. Refrigerate overnight and transport to the tailgate in a cooler. In a sealable plastic bag, add the confectioners' sugar and salt. Pack a metal bowl and whisk.

At the tailgate, about 30 minutes prior to eating, place the pan of crisp onto the grill over low heat. Turn the pan every 10 minutes to ensure that the crisp heats evenly. Remove from the grill.

To make the Bourbon Whipped Cream, combine the whipping cream mixture and sugar mixture in a metal bowl. Whisk in a circular motion until the cream forms soft peaks. Serve on the apple crisp.

Tailgaters at East Carolina in Greenville, North Carolina

Recipe Index

General Index